THE LORE OF
SAIL

THE LORE OF
SAIL

Facts On File Publications
460 Park Avenue South
New York, N.Y. 10016

THE LORE OF SAIL

Copyright©1982 by Nordbok, Gothenburg, Sweden.

Published in the United States of America in 1983 by
Facts on File, Inc., 460 Park Avenue South, New York, NY 10016.

Published in Sweden in 1983 by Nordbok, Gothenburg, Sweden.
Typeset by Bokstaven, Gothenburg, Sweden

Library of Congress Cataloging in Publication Data

Baker, William A.
    The lore of sail.

    Includes index.
    1. Sailing ships. I. Svensson, Sam II. Scheen,
Rolf III. Title.
VM145.B32 1984 623.8'223 83-1530

ISBN 0-87196-221-7

Printed in Spain 1983 by Novograph, S.A., Madrid

Contents

Introduction   7
Captain Sam Svensson

1 The Hull   15
William Avery Baker

Plans; midship sections; forebodies; tools; details of hulls;
afterbodies; rudders; steering gears; types of hulls; anchors;
windlasses; winches; davits; hatches; accommodations;
galley; pumps; lanterns.

2 Spars and Rigging   75
Captain Sam Svensson

Masts and spars; tops and crosstrees; stays and shrouds;
bowsprits; details of mainmast and mainyard; rigging of old
steamers.

3 The Sail   123
Captain Sam Svensson

Different sails; names of sails on various ships; the square
sail; the studding sail; patent reefing; different rigging of
lower square sails; the gaff sail; the gaff topsail; the staysail;
bonnets and reefs; bowlines and beatas; blocks; halliards and
sheets; tools for sail- and rig-making; types of sailing ships;
merchant flags; house flags; early flag-signalling; cordage;
wires; knots and whipping.

4 Navigation and Ship-handling   213
Rolf Scheen

Log, line and glass; the lead and line; old navigational
instruments; the octant and sextant; compass cards; the
traverse board; bearings; lighthouses; charts; the theory of
sailing; different courses; small-boat handling; wearing;
tacking; backing and filling; to heave to; mooring.

Index   253

INTRODUCTION
by Sam Svensson

F rom ancient times, sailing the seas has been a unique profession, with techniques and methods which have always puzzled the landlubber. One thousand years before Christ, Solomon said that the way of a ship in the midst of the sea was too wonderful for him to understand.

In our time, there have been radical technical developments. On the seas, ships as well as the life of the sailor have been changed to such a degree that no similarity whatsoever with the olden days exists. This may be why general interest in old nautical things and in the sailing ship in particular has grown to such an extent. People all over the world now want accurate data about the construction, equipment, and handling of old ships.

Long ago, ships were always built of wood, except in the case of even more primitive materials such as reed, skin, and bark; but these materials were only used for the most primitive sailing in narrow seas. Since ancient times, ships have been built according to two methods: carvel and clinker. The first method was developed in the eastern Mediterranean countries, where Egyptians, Phoenicians, and others built ships with outside planking ingeniously joined by being placed edge to edge. This art came into general use in Southern Europe, and during the Middle Ages it spread along the coast of Western Europe, reaching the Baltic during the latter part of the 15th century. It then became the dominant way of shipbuilding, and after the middle of the 16th century all large vessels were carvel-built.

During the latter half of the 17th century, however, when shipbuilding had become a science and ships could be theoretically designed in advance, larger and sturdier ships were being built. The pictures on pages 33 and 34 show constructional details of a large 18th-century ship. During the second half of the 19th century, when iron and steel were being used more generally for shipbuilding, there was a decline in shipbuilding in wood. The art survived longest in the United States, where large wooden merchant sailing vessels were built up to the time of the First World War. The four-masted bark *Roanoke* – 3,439 gross tons, built in 1892 – and the six-masted schooner, *Wyoming* – 3,730 tons, built in 1909 – indicate the size limits of wood used in constructing ships. In many other places,

GRACE DIEU, also known as GREAT HARRY

perhaps mostly in the Eastern Mediterranean and in the Near East, but also in the Baltic, small sailing vessels were built of wood well into the 20th century. In addition to carvel-built wooden ships, clinker-built vessels were also being constructed. This method originated in the Baltic where, even during the Viking Age, large clinker-built ships sailed to Iceland and Greenland. In the Middle Ages, the clinker-building method was predominant in Northern Europe, and many large ships were constructed. Perhaps one of the largest was Henry IV's ship *Grace Dieu,* built in 1418; she was almost fifty meters long and about twelve meters wide. She had a complicated treble-clinker planking. According to the clinker method, the planking was built first and the frames were inserted afterward. We know this because the wreck of the *Grace Dieu* was discovered near Southampton, and it showed that the rivets of the skin were clinched underneath the frames.

Experimental ships of iron were built during the first half of the 19th century, until, gradually, iron came into more general use. After 1850, England had several shipyards which built only iron

GREAT BRITAIN was the first screw steamer built for transatlantic service. Designed by Brunel, she was built in 1843 of iron. She measured 289 ft.×50 ft. and could accommodate 360 passengers. She was later converted into a sailing ship. Her hull lay for many years in South Georgia. She is now restored in Bristol, where she was built.

vessels. The introduction of the steam engine for propulsion also encouraged the use of iron as a shipbuilding material. The first iron ships were built according to the same principles as those used for wooden vessels, but as builders grew more experienced, special methods were adopted for the structure of iron ships. One early change was to provide the iron steamship with a double bottom and internal keel, instead of the former bar keel used in sailing vessels. The keelson was now placed on top of the floors. Longitudinal framing, which slowly came into use around 1900, also deviated from the kind of standard shipbuilding that had been used for a thousand years.

The steam engine and later the diesel engine have only been in existence for a very short time in the whole history of navigation. During most of this time, masts and sails were the only means of propulsion on long voyages. For ages, rigging consisted of one mast and one sail only, and it was not until the end of the Middle Ages that mechanical progress made it possible to construct better and more functional rigging. These developments continued for several centuries and reached their high

The steel-hulled ARCHIBALD RUSSELL was built in 1905, the last four-masted barque to be built for British owners (John Hardie of Glasgow). In 1924, she was sold to Gustaf Erikson of Mariehamn, Finland. At the outbreak of war in 1939, she was in Hull and was impounded by Britain. After the war, she was broken up.

point after the middle of the 19th century, when, due to competition from the steamship, shipyards turned out perfectly sparred and rigged sailing ships.

There have been many important phases in the history of rigging: such as setting a topsail above the original single square sail, using fidded topmasts that could be sent down, the footrope and the jackstay, which together revolutionized the work of handling sails, the introduction of wire, first for the standing rigging and then for the running gear, and, finally, mechanical aids for handling sails in large ships, such as patent sheaves and brace-and-halliard winches.

Flags are not only decorative but also useful. Originally, flags come from field banners carried in ancient battles. In comparison with the flags of ancient kings and military commanders, our national flags are of very recent date. The oldest national flag now in use is the Danish flag, according to a legend of 1219, and it was probably followed by the Swedish and Dutch flags. Among the flags of world powers, America has the oldest, dating in its present general form of stars and stripes from 1777. The French tricolor is dated 1794; the English flag in its present form is from 1801.

Pages 210-211 show the flags used by some of the old sailing ship companies. The Hanseatic League's red-and-white flag of the Middle Ages comes as number one on this list.

Once the oar had been invented, there were very early attempts to find some mechanical aid which could move ships in a calm or drive them against a head wind. But there was no mechanical power. Thus, it was not until the steam engine was invented and perfected to some degree that steam navigation got under way. The first ships of this type were used for river traffic in the United States, and also for coastal traffic around the British Isles.

Deep-sea fishing is fun, but it is also an important means of getting food. Of old, deep-sea fishing was always carried out in fishing craft fitted with sails. Well-known examples of such craft are the English fishing smacks on the North Sea banks and the American schooners on the Newfoundland coast.

Sailing as a sport has an old heritage. Caligula had pleasure boats in Lake Nemi, and the Doge of Venice had a luxurious galley which he used every year in the ceremony of marrying himself to the sea. In ancient times, pleasure sailing was a sport reserved for kings and men of rank only. During the 19th century, it began to occupy more and more industrialists and businessmen, and, gradually, sailing as a sport has reached the widespread popularity of our own time. Today, there are yacht clubs in all countries where there is access to navigable waters. In order to standardize rules for yachting competitions, a great many so-called one-design boats have been constructed, boats which are built according to accurate measurements and regulations so that they will be exactly alike; thus it will be mostly the skill of the helmsman that decides the race. Yacht-racing courses are also decided according to an international standard.

As long as man has sailed the ocean, he has struggled for supremacy on the sea. Even in ancient times, a variety of ships were built specifically for war or trade; nevertheless, merchant ships have been used in war and warships in commerce down through the years. As the nations were industrialized, diversity according to function became more noticeable.

It might be said that navigation is the sailor's theory and seamanship his practice. The sounding lead is the sailor's oldest instrument; recognition of the coastline his only way of piloting. In deep waters and when land was out of sight this simple method of navigation was useless. Before the compass was invented, the sailor had to find his way by observations that would indicate a definite direction: the movement of the sun and stars, the direction of the wind and how the clouds were drifting, changes in ocean swell, the flight of birds and how the fish swam. On a long voyage not even the compass was a sufficient guide, so that such trips could not be undertaken until astronomic navigation had been discovered. Even then, for hundreds of years the only means by which a sailor could measure the sun's meridian height was with a simple instrument which determined latitude. The ability to make longitudinal calculations came at a much later date. For that purpose the navigator required Hadley's octant or a sextant, as well as a chronometer and complete nautical tables, or if there were no chronometer, he had to be able to calculate the longitude by means of lunar distances. As in other fields, electronics now does most of the work formerly done by astronomic navigation.

Previously, seamanship could be defined as the care and handling of sailing ships. Page 249 illustrates a portion of this almost forgotten art: how a brig can be put to sea against the wind by backing and filling downriver. Today, a vessel is guided by means of the rudder and the screw. The art of guiding a power-driven vessel has been mastered by many of today's seamen, but skill in sailing is rarely to be found. *The Lore of Sail* has tried to recover some small part of this forgotten art.

The first chapter of
The Lore of Sail deals
with the hull and
some of its more im-
portant details. The

next page shows a
sketch of Columbus'
ship, the SANTA
MARIA.

THE HULL
by W.A. Baker

Throughout history, the shape of ships' hulls has been determined by the materials and methods of construction, means of propulsion, use, fashion, and whim. Primitive craft still range in form from the round (woven baskets, skin-covered frameworks, and even pottery) to the long and narrow (bundles of reeds and shaped logs). Quite early on, the Egyptians sewed wooden planks together to produce flat-bottomed boats having the proportions of their reed craft. Other ancient peoples learned to improve the hollowed-out log canoe by spreading it open and adding one or more planks on each side. For centuries, built-up hulls followed the general shape of such canoes.

The continued existence of primitive craft in various parts of the world serves to emphasize the regions where major sea-going types of vessels developed – the Mediterranean basin, northern Europe, and China. Through most of recorded history, there was a parallel development of the two basic hull forms noted above, the "round" ship or bulky cargo carrier and the "long" ship built for speed. Shipbuilding history is concerned mainly with wooden oar-propelled and sailing vessels; metal ships and mechanical propulsion are relatively recent developments.

Two basic techniques have been employed in the construction of wooden vessels, the "shell" and the "skeleton", and combinations of them can be found as early as the 7th century. In the first, the planking is secured together and supporting frames added; in the second, as the term implies, a framework is erected to which the planking is fastened. The frames of a vessel built by the shell method take their shapes from the assembled planking while the planking of a skeleton-built ship must follow the predetermined shape of the frames. A possible explanation of the transition from the older shell technique to the skeleton is the retention in the hull of moulds erected to guide the shaping of the planking. Perhaps the earliest evidence of the skeleton method of construction is an early 14th-century painting showing Italian shipbuilders at work.

The features of early built-up vessels were the result of materials and tools employed. Early Scandinavian shipbuilders, for example, used the axe and adze to shape one long plank from each half of a split log. The planks so fashioned were lapped at the edges and secured together by withes or animal sinews (later by metal rivets); this is basically the present-day clinker planking. When a suitable number of planks had been fastened to each other and to the stem and sternpost, supporting frames were added which were held in place by lashings to lugs that had been left on the planks during the original shaping. Experts do not fully agree on the origin of the Viking ship. Some believe it developed from the skin boat when thin planks replaced sewn skins on a flexible framework but others favor the descent from the distended log canoe to which planks were added. The midsection of the famous Gokstad ship, *circa* 900 A.D., page 26, shows a late example of lashed-on planking; the lower eight planks were lashed to the frames while the upper planks were nailed.

Shipbuilders in ancient Egypt employed the saw to produce several planks from each log. The usual native woods, acacia and sycamore, were obtainable only in relatively short lengths which led Herodotus to liken the construction of an Egyptian ship to the building of a brick wall. In preserved vessels the planks were fastened edge to edge by various combinations of dowels or tenons, recessed dovetail pieces, and lashings which produced the smooth outside finish now called carvel planking. Being primarily river craft, Egyptian ships often had only a thick plank instead of a structural keel. Some types, built without frames, had arc-shaped midsections and were kept from spreading by deck beams that protruded through the planking. Large versions of Egyptian flat-bottomed boats had widely-spaced supporting frames and it is now believed that the larger round-bottomed vessels also had them. A prominent feature on many Egyptian vessels was a heavy rope truss, fitted from bow to stern, to keep the ends from drooping.

Available information indicates that Phoenician, Greek, and Roman ships were basically double-enders and that their builders, who employed the shell technique, had a sound knowledge of the structure needed in seagoing vessels. Records of numbers of Roman warships constructed in short periods of time, 220 ships in three months in 254 A.D., imply the use of some sort of moulds to achieve duplication of these shell-built vessels. The Romans had three basic types of vessels – chubby sailing merchantmen, stout warships propelled by oars and

PROFILE OF A WOODEN SAILING SHIP, 1864

This semi-clipper ship was constructed in 1862 by Niels Kierkegaard, naval architect and Master Shipwright at the Old Shipyard in Gothenburg. In 1864, he published a handbook on naval architecture which contained drawings of eighteen different ships, including this one. His example was followed by shipbuilders all over Scandinavia. The ship shown here has concave bows with narrow waterlines and a lean run under the transom counter and surmounting square stern. She was rigged as a bark, as indicated by the three shrouds and single back stay in the mizzen rigging and shown by the chain plates. All the chain plates are bolted flat to the side of the ship without any channels. They go through the main rail, so the deadeyes will be located inside the topgallant bulwark. The fore and main

*rigging has four lower
shrouds, two topmast
backstays, one
topgallant backstay,
and one royal
backstay, as indicated
by the chain plates.
This same ship is
shown on pages 22
and 23.*

1	Sternpost
2	Keel
3	False keel or shoe
4	Fore foot, gripe
5	Stem
6	Headpiece
7	Garboard strake
8	Bottom planking
9	Side planking
10	Wale
11	Sheer strake
12	Covering board
13	Bulwark

14	Rough-tree rail
15	Topgallant bul-wark
16	Rudder
17	Counter
18	Stern
19	Chain plates
20	Cathead
21	Figurehead
22	Mizzenmast
23	Mainmast
24	Foremast
25	Bowsprit

used for ramming in sea battles, and light speedy galleys for carrying messages and important persons.

From Roman times to about 1200 A.D., there was little change in the shapes of Mediterranean ships. The merchant sailing vessels remained double-enders with rather full sterns and they were still steered by heavy side oars. Following the earlier practice deck beam ends protruded through the carvel planking and were secured to heavy fore-and-aft wales. "Castles", not part of the hull, were fixed prominently on bow and stern, the light square work of house carpenters contrasting with the sturdy curved work of the shipwrights. One important change was the shift from the Roman square rig to a two-or-three-masted lateen rig for the majority of the merchant vessels, although the older rig continued to exist.

From the time of the first Crusade in 1095, when northern European vessels in large numbers entered the Mediterranean, the features of Northern and Southern "round" ships slowly mingled. By then, in the north, the typical Viking ships had been superseded by double-ended sailing vessels in which the clinker planking, high stem and sternpost, and side rudder persisted. These vessels became wider in proportion to length and deeper; they were fitted with a single deck supported inside the hull but a few heavy tie beams protruded through the planking. Small castles appeared on the bow and stern which became more substantial as time passed. Stern rudders were first used during the second half of the 12th century. Southern builders also adopted the stern rudder and returned to the square rig for their larger ships.

The more or less standard merchant ship type that resulted from the mingling of features, commonly called the cog, was employed from the Mediterranean to the Baltic into the early 15th century. The cog was basically a double-ender whose after body seems to have been fuller than her forebody. Her straight sternpost that carried the rudder had little rake; her stem, which had considerable rake forward, was usually straight in the north and curved in the south. The forecastle, triangular in plan, projected over the stem but its after end was partially faired into the hull. The stern castle was an angular house whose after corners overhung the sharp stern. The standard rig was one mast with a single square sail; the first addition to this rig seems to have been a lateen mizzen to improve steering balance. Still there were readily apparent differences between the Northern and Southern cogs. The former had clinker planking, a few projecting tie beams, and decks supported inside the hull, while cogs of the Mediterranean region had carvel planking with all deck beams protruding and secured to wales. Pictorial evidence for details of Northern cogs was substantiated in 1962 when a nearly complete 14th-century cog was found in the River Weser at Bremen.

Western historians, in concentrating their studies on the nations of the Mediterranean basin, tend to overlook the activities of Chinese seamen who from about 700 to 1500 A.D. probably were the world leaders in ocean shipping. There were well-documented voyages to Africa's east coast in the 14th and 15th centuries in ships that were about 200 feet long, had four or more masts, and carried complements of several hundred persons. There is a strong probability that Chinese ships sailed westward around the Cape of Good Hope and into the South Atlantic before 1459, nearly twenty years before the Portuguese rounded the Cape eastbound.

The origins of Chinese vessels are lost in time but it is thought that knowledge of shipbuilding was brought by colonists who came into China from the West. Some 20th-century types on the upper Yangtze River are practically identical with Egyptian craft of 1600 B.C. A Chinese treatise of 1119 A.D. likened the hull shape of the biggest ships to a rectangular grain measure that had sloping sides and ends and described a matting sail that moved around its mast like a door on a hinge. Marco Polo's descriptions of Chinese vessels at the end of the 13th century are well known; some information about Chinese ships may have reached Europe earlier through Arab traders. Far in advance of western technology, Chinese shipbuilders produced vessels with numerous transverse watertight bulkheads which are thought to have been inspired by the bamboo, centerline balanced rudders by the 1st century of our era, and leeboards by the mid-8th century. After the 15th-century African voyages official Chinese maritime activities were reduced to the minimum necessary to protect coastal shipping. Some types of vessels developed by that time probably have changed little

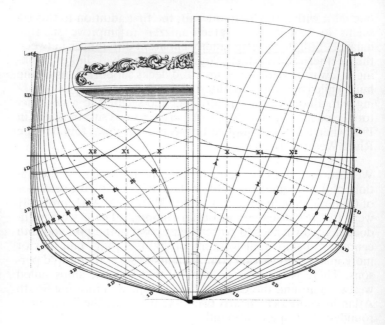

LINES OF A WOODEN SAILING SHIP OF 500 TONS DWT, 1864

The shape of the hull is determined by three sets of planes drawn at right angles to each other. Horizontal planes are called water lines, where they intersect the hull. They are shown as straight lines in A and as curves in B. WL indicates the load water line. Vertical planes going fore and aft and parallel to the longitudinal middle-line plane are called buttocks. Their intersections with the ship's hull are shown in A as curved lines, marked X, X1, and X2. Vertical planes going across the hull show the curves of the sides of the ship's transverse frame lines. Their shape is given in the body plan above, which shows an end view of the hull. The frame lines are numbered in the afterbody and lettered in the forebody. The body plan also gives the diagonal lines extending from the middle-line plane. The diagonal intersections with the surface of the hull are drawn (opposite) in C. D (opposite) gives the deck plan: three hatches, a fo'c'sle for 10 sailors, galley, and sail locker in the deckhouse, while the cabinhouse holds the captain's cabin, the mates' rooms, saloon, messroom, and pantries. The little house furthest aft holds the lamp locker and the officers' lavatory.

A

W L

B

C

D

since; other types are known to have been influenced by foreign contacts. The variations of proportions and details are almost impossible to catalog but all are well-suited to local conditions.

During the 15th century, European seagoing ships grew larger until Northern shipbuilders eventually realized that there was a limit to the size of successful clinker-built ships. The largest known, the *Grace Dieu* built in England in 1418, was a failure and sailed only from Southampton to the Hamble estuary near Bursledon where she was struck by lightning and burned in 1439. Projecting deck and tie beams, difficult to make watertight, were abandoned and the larger European ships became a combination of Northern and Southern features – smooth planking generally hung on pre-erected framing with inside supported decks. Today, it is difficult to describe accurately some of the ship types that followed the cog, such as the galleon, galleass, and galiot derived from the proportions of oar-propelled vessels, and the hulk, carrack, and caravel, the bulky cargo ships.

During the 15th and 16th centuries, the above-water appearance of European ships' hulls changed considerably. Castles remained large but lost their angular look and were merged into the main hull. Around 1550, large ships were given a square stern that provided better support to the superstructure than the medieval round stern. About the same time the forecastle lost its triangular form; its projection was dropped to form a beakhead below the bowsprit in imitation of the galley's ram. The major ship type for the next 75 to 100 years was the galleon, which had less sheer and lower superstructure than earlier types and was narrower in proportion to length.

During the 17th century, there was considerable change in framing details. Up to the late 16th century, the single frame of several naturally curved pieces with scarfed joints was standard for almost all sizes of vessels. Such joints were weak and one improvement was to shift the pieces so that they overlapped each other side by side for several feet. The lowest pieces, the floor timbers, were nearly square in section and were spaced along the keel about their own thickness apart. In way of the overlapping there was nearly solid timber for the length of the ship; the pieces of framing were not fastened together but were held in place by the outside planking and inside sheathing. By the early 18th century, the pieces had been extended to butt against each other and were fastened together to form complete frames that could be erected as units. This is essentially the pattern of framing still employed in the building of large wooden ships. Space does not permit descriptions of the various combinations of double full and single filling frames used in the intervening years.

The rough semicircular shape of the log canoe was poor for stability but builders soon learned that it could be improved by flattening the bottom of the log. In general, a flattened semicircle would be a simple description of the underwater midsection shape of nearly all vessels until the early part of the 18th century. The unusual V-shape of the Viking ships remained a local Scandinavian feature. Radical changes in the underwater forms of ships came in the 18th and 19th centuries.

The earliest preserved ship plans and treatises on shipbuilding date from the early 1400s. Written in Italian, they describe Mediterranean practices and indicate a long tradition of ship design using arcs of circles and their derivatives to shape hulls and their parts. Succeeding works from other countries amplify the details and show that hull proportions and parts were defined in terms of breadth or keel length, usually the former. Vessels built for fast sailing differed from bulky carriers more in relation of length to breadth than in the shape of the sections. In 1750, and perhaps even later, it was still possible to design a satisfactory ship with no tools but a pair of compasses and a straight-edge.

About 1670, the results of what perhaps were the first systematic ship resistance experiments were recorded in England. Other scientific studies followed, particularly in France, where the first treatise on stability was published in 1746.

In the 18th century, many legal and extra-legal operations required the use of small fast-sailing vessels. Those built first on Jamaica and later on Bermuda and the shores of Chesapeake Bay became world-famous. The terms Virginia-built or Virginia-model became almost synonymous with speed; by the early 19th century the type was known as the Baltimore clipper.

(After the Gokstad ship.) The ship is clinker-built from oak, with 16 boards on each side, and has a large keelson, and a deep keel for sailing.

1 Keel
2 Keelson
3 Floors
4 Futtocks
5 Toptimber
6 Clinker-built skin
7 Flooring
8 Mast partners
9 Riders to keep mast partners in place
10 Gallows

MIDSHIP SECTION OF A VIKING SHIP, MIDDLE OF 9TH CENTURY

The lower eight boards are tied to the ribs through cleats that are left on each board-plank. The rest of the boards are nailed. The ship is un-decked, but has a flat floor, on top of which a very heavy mast partner runs over six of the beams. The high gallows make it possible to erect a large tent on board. There are no rowing-benches. The oarsmen probably sat on loose benches or sea-chests.

(Opposite)
A *Wooden ship*
1 Keel
2 Garboard strake

3 Bottom planking
4 Bends or wales
5 Topside planking
6 Sheer strake
7 Floor
8 2nd futtock
9 4th futtock
10 Long toptimber
11 Limbers, water course
12 Keelson
13 Limber board
14 Limber strake
15 Floor ceiling
16 Thick strakes of ceiling
17 Air courses
18 Lower deck hanging knee
19 Lower deck shelf
20 Lower deck clamp
21 Hold stanchion
22 Lower deck beam

23 Lower deck, lower deck planking
24 Lower deck waterway
25 Lower deck spirketing
26 Tween deck ceiling
27 Upper deck hanging knee
28 Upper deck shelf
29 Upper deck clamp
30 Tween deck stanchion
31 Upper deck beam
32 Upper deck, upper deck planking
33 Upper deck waterway
34 Covering board
35 Bulwark stanchions
36 Plank sheer

WOODEN AND WOOD AND IRON VESSEL

MIDSHIP SECTION OF TWO DIFFERENT SHIPS, SECOND HALF OF THE 19TH CENTURY

37 Bulwark planking	16 Covering board	31 Upper deck tie plate
38 Main rail	17 Bilge stringer	
39 Tween decks	18 Cargo battens (in hold)	32 Upper deck stringer plate
40 Hold	19 Hold pillar; hold stanchion	33 Upper deck waterway
B *Composite ship (wooden vessel with iron frames)*	20 Lower deck	34 Covering board
	21 Lower deck beam	35 Bulwark stanchion
1 False keel or shoe	22 Bracket end (of lower deck beam)	36 Main rail
2 Keel	23 Lower deck tie plate	37 Topgallant bulwark stanchion
3 Garboard strake	24 Lower deck stringer	
4 Keel plate	25 Lower deck waterway	38 Topgallant rail
5 Frame		39 Deadeye
6 Floor	26 Cargo battens (between decks)	40 Upper channel
7 Limbers	27 Upper deck pillar, upper deck stanchion	41 Bulwark planking
8 Reverse frame		42 Chainplate
9 Side intercostal keelson	28 Upper deck	43 Planksheer
10 Center line keelson	29 Upper deck beam	44 Sheer strake
11 Limber boards	30 Bracket end (of upper deck beam)	45 Iron sheer strake
12 Ceiling		46 Lower channel
13 Side keelson		47 Chain bolt
14 Bilge keelson		48 Preventer bolt
15 Bilge plate		

27

A major feature of the type was a return to the V-shaped bottom of the Viking ship, the so-called rising floor, which for a time was adopted for large ships whenever speed was more important than cargo capacity.

Baltimore clippers were tried in the East India and China trades but their speed could not overcome their limited cargo capacity, a result of their V-shaped underbodies. The best ships in the China trade had a modified packet ship form. The clipper ship era, which began in the mid-1840s, ended in the United States in 1857 and in England about 1870. The large, extreme clippers developed out of a rising fashion for speed and publicity that was exaggerated by the discovery of gold in California and Australia. Speed at any cost prevailed over cargo capacity. Successful clippers were built with both rising and flat floors although the faster ships tended toward the latter as the era progressed. Few had the hollow water-lines popularly associated with the type, the average being more like those shown on pages 22 and 23. Clipper ship speeds were very largely the result of hard driving made possible by their larger size. Economic pressures finally forced a return to the best of the packet ship forms, ships nearly as fast but capable of carrying more cargo.

The presence of figures of animals, gods, and goddesses on ships can be traced into antiquity; the latter two probably were used more to ensure divine protection than as decoration. The Vikings fitted fierce dragon heads on their ships to frighten their enemies. About 1600, there began a period of over a century of elaborate ship decoration on both merchant and warships in the form of stern and quarter galleries embellished with carvings, carved panels along the sides, large figureheads, and complicated head structures. By 1800, these had been reduced to some stern windows with a few carvings around them on the transom, small quarter galleries, and relatively simple head structures.

The introduction of successful commercial steam propulsion in the early 19th century brought new problems to shipbuilders – the concentrated weight of the machinery and the stresses induced by the paddle-wheels or the screw propeller. Until the end of their days, paddle-wheel steamers from European shipyards had their paddle-boxes constructed as appendages to the hull. Except on ocean-going vessels builders in the United States carried the superstructures out to a line that enclosed the paddle-boxes.

Until about 1870, ocean-going steamships had the general form and construction of the sailing ship and, because of the unreliability of steam machinery, carried large sailing rigs. Sails for emergency use did not entirely disappear until nearly World War I.

By the middle of the 19th century, further resistance experiments and practical experience with steam propulsion had shown that fine lines were necessary for speed. A sailing ship could add sail to overcome poor lines, but early steam machinery was limited in power and breakdowns were frequent, occasionally with disastrous results.

Although a few iron parts had been used on wooden ships as far back as 1675, commercial iron shipbuilding did not start until the 1830s. Early practice was to have an iron structural member similar to every wooden part, which can be seen by comparing the sections shown on pages 27 and 30. Many shipowners were prejudiced against iron and before it was fully adopted there was the interim phase of the composite ship in which iron framing and tie plates were used with wood planking and decking, as shown on page 27.

As shipbuilders gained experience with iron vessels they learned that the longitudinal material could be distributed to better advantage than in wooden ships in which the keel was considered the backbone that provided most of the strength. It was soon realized that a metal ship should be built as a girder with as much strength in the deck as in the bottom. This, of course, is modern shipbuilding practice. Steel, which is now practically the universal material in all large ships, began to replace iron about 1870. Lightweight metals, particularly aluminium, are finding wide employment in the construction of superstructures on large ships and the entire hulls of yachts and other small vessels.

Chemical resins and glass fibers are now standard materials for the construction of yachts, small commercial craft, and even

SOME CONSTRUCTION DETAILS OF WOODEN SHIPS, 19TH CENTURY

A *The timbers were placed at right angles to the keel, except at the ends, both fore and aft, where they were placed at right angles to the ship's side. These frames were called cant timbers.*

B *To make the plank strakes run fair, fore and aft, the midship bend (ab) was divided into the same number of planks as the frames (ac) and as at the ends of the ship (ad).*

C *At the ends of the ship, if the planks were too wide, stealers (a) were put in between them; if too narrow, they were formed as joggle planks (b).*

D *Below the water line tree nails (trunnels) and bolts were used to fasten the planking to the frames in addition to two nails in each plank butt.*

1 Tree nail
2 Bolt
3 Nail

DETAILS OF A WOODEN VESSEL (FROM PAASCH)

A, B
  Horizontal section of bow
1 Stem
2 Stem rabbet
3 Apron
4 Eking
5 Deck hook
6 Deck hook bolts
7 Stem piece
8 Knight head
9 Hawse timbers
10 Fore cant timbers
11 Outside plank

12 Ceiling plank
13 Breast hook
14 Breast hook bolts
15 Deck beam
C *Deck and hatchway*
1 Hatch cover
2 Hatchway
3 Hatchway coamings
4 Hatchway carling
5 Head ledges
6 Fore and after
7 Hatch end beams

8 Half beams
9 Lodging knees
10 Deck stanchions
11 Mast hole
12 Mast carlings
13 Chocks *(12 and 13 forming mast partners)*
14 Mast beams
15 Deck planking

some naval vessels up to about 150 feet in length. Ferro-cement or steel reinforced concrete is a low-cost material that can be used by semi-skilled labor to produce yachts and small commercial vessels.

The worldwide energy crisis of the early 1970s has turned the thoughts of some seafarers to a renewed use of the winds for propulsion in some cargo-carrying services. This does not imply a return to the old-time sailing ship but rather a development of new hulls and rigs. Although the day of the wooden commercial ship is past and in some parts of the world wood is in limited supply even for the construction of pleasure boats, there is a growing interest by young and old in learning and preserving the traditional handcrafts associated with the art of wooden shipbuilding.

LONGITUDINAL SECTION OF THE AFTERBODY OF A 40-GUN FRIGATE, 1768

1	Keel	13 Mizzenmast	24 Doorway to
2	Floors	14 Mast step	quarter gallery
3	Keelson	15 Orlop deck beams	25 Wardroom
4	Sternpost	16 Gun deck beams	26 Storerooms
5	Inner post	17 Upper deck	27 Ballast
6	Stern knee	beams	28 Water, beer casks
7	Deadwood	18 Poop deck beams	29 Salt meat
8	Crutches	19 Main capstan	30 Powder room
9	Rudder	20 Gunports	31 Lantern for
10	Tiller	21 Companion hood	powder room
11	Wheel	22 Officer's room	32 Shot locker
12	Binnacle	23 Great cabin	

LONGITUDINAL SECTION OF THE FOREBODY OF A 40-GUN FRIGATE, 1768

1 Keel	12 Head rails	21 Kevels
2 Floors	13 Foremast	22 Knight
3 Keelson	14 Mast step	23 Jeer capstan
4 Forefoot	15 Breast hooks	24 Galley
5 Gripe	16 Bitts	25 Cable
6 Stem	17 Orlop deck	26 Mangerboard
7 Apron	beams	27 Shotlocker
8 Stemson	18 Gun deck beams	28 Galley wood
9 Bobstay piece	19 Upper deck	29 Bosun's stores
10 Filling chocks	beams	30 Cable tier
11 Head timbers	20 Cathead	

THREE-MASTED BARK, LONGITUDINAL SECTION OF THE AFTERBODY

1	Keel	12	Pinrail	19	Ceiling
2	False keel or shoe	13	Main rail	20	Tween deck beams
3	Keel scarf	14	Topgallant bulwark	21	Crutches
4	Floor	15	Lamp locker, roundhouse	22	Mizzenmast
5	Keelson	16	Cabin house	23	Rudder
6	Keelson scarf	17	Main deck beams		
7	Stern knee	18	Diagonal deck beam hanging knees		
8	After deadwood				
9	Inner post				
10	Sternpost				
11	Bearding line				

35

THREE-MASTED WOODEN SHIP, 500 TONS DWT, LONGITUDINAL SECTION OF THE FOREBODY

1	False keel or shoe	15	Kevel head	28	Bowsprit
2	Keel	16	Pawl bitt	29	Foreward bitt
3	Floors	17	Standard knee	30	Main deck beams
4	Keelson	18	Pawls	31	Tween deck ceiling
5	Fore deadwood	19	Pawl rim	32	Main deck diagonal hanging knees
6	Keel scarf	20	Windlass barrel		
7	Fore foot	21	Carrick bitt or windlass bitt	33	Tween deck beams
8	Cutwater piece, gripe	22	Mooring bollards	34	Lower hold ceiling
9	Stem	23	Pinrail	35	Breast hooks
10	Apron	24	Main rail	36	Foremast
11	Stemson	25	Topgallant rail		
12	Stem knee	26	Port		
13	Lace piece	27	Fore hatch coaming		
14	Cathead				

CARPENTER'S TOOLS, 1691

1 English broad axe
2 Folding rule, a foot and a half long
3 Horse iron with an iron handle
4 Reeming iron
5 Curved caulking iron
6 Carpenter's hatchet
7 Inside calipers
8 Dutch brace and bit
9 Small bevel
10 English auger with a screw
11 Dutch handsaw
12 English chisel
13 Gouge
14 Chalk line and reel
15 English adze
16 Draw knife
17 Chisel with a handle

CARPENTER'S TOOLS, 1691

1 Pair of pincers
2 Dutch rule
3 Caulking iron
4 Adze, as seen from the side
5 Big mallet with iron hoops
6 Crab iron

7 Spike iron
8 Crab iron, made like a clasp knife
9 Swedish chopping axe
10 Swedish adze
11 Dutch axe

12 Compass saw
13 Sledge hammer
14 Deck scraper
15 Rave hook or ripping iron for cleaning caulking from seams
16 English handsaw

38

17 Caulking iron	23 Grease well to use when caulking	27 English caulking mallet
18 Making iron		28 Common hammer
19 Compasses with crayon	24 Crowbar	
20 Dividers	25 English claw hammer	29 Reeming iron
21 Swedish auger	26 English auger with a wooden handle	30 Swedish gouge for pinewood
22 Small gouge to start auger holes		

ANCIENT RUDDERS

A   *Rudder arrangement in a Roman merchant ship about A.D. 200*
1   Stern ornament
2   Helmsmen
3   Tillers
4   Rudder stock
5   Sternpost
6   Carrying ropes
7   Lashing

8   Balcony
9   Rudder blade
B   *Tiller of the Viking ship from Gokstad, about A.D. 850*
C   *Rudder arrangement in the Viking era (Gokstad ship)*

1   Broadside view of steering oar
2   Stern view of steering oar
3   Tiller
4   Rudder rope
5   Knot
6   "Wart"
7   Tilting rope
8   Collar

B

C

RUDDERS

A	*Rudder in a wooden sailing ship*	5 Pintle straps	B	*Iron rudder*
1	Rudder blade	6 Pintles	1	Stock of rudder
2	Tiller	7 Gudgeon straps	2	Pintles
3	Rudder head		3	Rudder frame
4	Rudder stock		4	Heel pintle
			5	Rudder plate

C *Rudder of a Dutch fleut, middle of 17th century*
1 Tiller
2 Pintle straps
3 Rudder braces or gudgeon straps
4 Rudder blade
5 Sternpost
D *Rudder of small medieval ship*
1 Main piece of rudder
2 Back piece
3 Head
4 Tiller
5 Pintles
6 Pintle straps
7 Gudgeon straps

SOME STEERING GEARS

A *Steering arrange-
   ment in a big ship
   of the 17th cen-
   tury, when the
   rudder was con-
   trolled by a verti-
   cal lever called
   the whipstaff*
1 Rudder
2 Tiller
3 Whipstaff
4 Platform for the
   quartermaster
5 Hood for the
   quartermaster
6 Mizzenmast

B	*Common steering gear in elevation and plan of small wooden sailing ship, 19th century*		*tion of big steel sailing ship, latter part of 19th century*	8	Wheel box with side seats
1	Rudder	1	Rudder stock	9	Wheel gratings
2	Tiller	2	Stuffing box on deck	10	Log reel slung underneath wheel box
3	Wheel stand	3	Emergency tiller		
4	Tiller chain	4	Cross head	D	*Steering wheel from sailing ship, middle of the 19th century*
5	Barrel or drum	5	Coupling rods		
6	Wheel	6	Screw spindle-threaded right and left		
C	*Mechanical screw steering gear in plan and eleva-*	7	Wheel		

A The flower of the English hawthorn on the *Mayflower,* 1620 (from replica built in 1957)

B Stern of the Dutch pinnace *Dromedarus,* middle of the 17th century (from a model)

C Head ornament of the three-masted fore-and-aft schooner *Ellen* of Skärhamn, built at Thurö in 1908

D Name board of the Finnish barkentine *Ida,* wrecked on the west coast of Sweden in 1875

D

E Stern ornament of the three-masted fore-and-aft schooner *Meta-Jan* of Skive, Denmark

DECORATION

With most people illiterate, the name of a ship was often depicted by painted carvings on the stern (for example A *and* B)

Stern of the French ship *Le Soleil Royal*, built at Brest in 1669

FIGUREHEADS AND
CARVINGS

A   *Unidentified
wood carving, c.
1820*

B   *Figurehead of
unknown vessel,
from the middle
of the 19th cen-
tury*

C   *Name-board of
the* ALBION, *19th
century*

D   *Unidentified
figurehead, c.
1850*

E   *Unidentified car-
ving, c. 1850*

F   *Figurehead of the*
HORATIO, *1807*

49

A

A Chinese junk with a painted eye on her bow, known as oculus decoration.

"Suppose no eye no can see," the Chinese seaman says in his pidgin English. Such

painted eyes may also be seen on fishing craft in the Mediterranean.

B

C

B Dutch pinnace from the middle of the 17th century, with a painted waveline for a water line, to give an impression of speed. (Sketch from a model.)

C Brigantine from the middle of the 19th century, with painted ports on her sides. This painting was originally intended to make the ship look like a man-of-war, but later it remained as decoration only.

D Sculptured lion's head on gun-port lid, perhaps intended to put heart in the crew and to frighten the enemy: the Swedish ship *Wasa*, 1628

E Figurehead, from the 18th century

ANCHORS AND ANCHOR GEAR

A *Arrangement for fishing an anchor*
1 Pendant with fish tackle
2 Cathead
3 Chain cable
B *Chain cable*
1 Shackle
2 Stud link
3 Swivel

C, D *Hawser bends*
E *Grapnel*
F *Iron-stocked anchor*
G *Trotman's anchor*
H *Inglefield's anchor*

I *Cathead with anchor gear*
1 Anchor
2 Cable
3 Shackle
4 Cathead
5 Releasing gear
6 Cathead stopper
J *Mushroom anchor*
K *Hall's anchor*

ANCHORS

A	*Common anchor*	4	Shank	B	*Part of tree trunk with branches, used as an anchor*
1	Anchor ring	5	Crown		
2	Stock	6	Arm		
3	Hoops of the anchor stock	7	Fluke		
		8	Pea or bill		

C *Anchor, made
from tree
branches and
stone*

D *Roman anchor of
Caligula from
Lake Nemi*

E *Viking anchor
from the Oseberg
ship*

55

WINDLASS AND CAPSTAN

A *Windlass*
1. Pawl bitt
2. Windlass bitts
3. Cheeks of windlass bitts
4. Standard knees
5. Warping heads
6. Windlass barrel with whelps
7. Strongback
8. Crosshead
9. Purchase rod
10. Pawl
11. Pawl rim
12. Purchase rims

B *Old windlass*
1. Windlass bitt
2. Cheek of windlass bitts
3. Bolts
4. Windlass barrel
5. Bar holes

C *Method of heaving anchor with a messenger*
1. Cable
2. Cathead
3. Nippers
4. Messenger (an endless rope)
5. Capstan
6. Capstan bars

D *Capstan*
1. Head
2. Bar holes
3. Barrel
4. Whelps

E *Capstan*
1. Drumhead
2. Capstan-bar holes
3. Barrel
4. Whelps
5. Whelp chocks
6. Pawls
7. Pawl rim
8. Capstan partners
9. Deck planking

57

WINDLASS AND WINCH

A *Patent steam windlass*

1 Levers, hand-power levers
2 Crosshead
3 Warping heads
4 Side bitts
5 Bearing caps
6 Screwbrake nuts
7 Wildcats (Gypsies)
8 Windlass barrel or drum
9 Main cone driving wheels
10 Crosshead bracket
11 Cable relievers
12 Chain pipes
13 Bandbrakes
14 Cylinders
15 Steampipe flange
16 Valve casings
17 Bedplate

C

B **Steam winch**
1 Warping heads or gypsy heads
2 Winch drum
3 Main cogwheel
4 Reversing link
5 Pinion shaft cogwheel
6 Clutch lever
7 Cylinders
8 Slide-valve box
9 Steam exhaust pipe
10 Inlet steampipe
11 Tie rod, stay
12 Throttle valve
13 Reversing lever
14 Drum shaft bearing
15 Connecting rod
16 Bedplate
17 Piston rod and crosshead
18 Crank pin
19 Combined gear- and flywheel
20 Strap-brake pedal
21 Weigh shaft

C *The four-masted barquentine* MOZART, *built in 1904 at Greenock for German ownership. Her registered dimensions were 260 ft. × 40.5 ft. and she had a gross tonnage of 2,005. She was very up-to-date in design, and besides being fitted with water ballast tanks, she was given such labour-saving devices as halliard and brace winches, steam-powered by a donkey boiler. In 1922, she was sold to Hugo Lundguist of Mariehamn, Finland, and she spent her last years sailing the Australian route. She was broken up in 1936.*

A

B

BELL AND HOURGLASS

A A little bell placed aft, on which the helmsman struck the time, and which was repeated by the lookout at the main bell

B Hourglass, measuring half an hour. Each glass on board accounts for half an hour, and is sounded by one stroke of the bell; each watch of four hours is divided into eight glasses, corresponding to eight bells. The six watches are: the 1st watch 20–24, the 2nd watch (middle watch) 00–04, the day watch (morning watch) 04–08, the forenoon watch 08–12, the noon watch 12–16, and the afternoon watch 16–20. Three bells thus mean that the time is 01.30, 05.30, 09.30, 13.30, 17.30, or 21.30. Eight bells mean that a watch is over. The number of glasses is struck on the bell as a series of double strokes. For instance, 15.30 (seven glasses): ++ ++ ++ +

WHISTLES AND BELL

A Boatswain's call
B Fog horn made from a bullock's horn
C Fog horn of copper
D A bell hanging in a belfry, Nelson's VICTORY
E Admiral Nelson's flagship at Trafalgar, 1805, was VICTORY, launched in 1765. She was a first-rate ship of the line with three gun-decks and 102 guns. Her crew totalled 850 men. She is one of the few preserved wooden warships in Great Britain, where she lies at Portsmouth.

D

E

GALLEY

A *Ship's galley, according to Chapman, 1768*
1 Pea-soup kettle
2 Brick fireplace
3 Galley stacks

B *Brick fireplace on board the Swedish ship Wasa, 1628. There was no chimney and the smoke had to find its way out wherever it could.*

C *Open sheet-iron fireplace, on the deck of a coaster in the Indian Ocean*

D *Big galley stove, from the beginning of the 20th century*

65

ACCOMMODATIONS

Up to the middle of the 17th century the crew had no special accommodations but had to sleep on the bare deck or find a place for themselves. Meals were eaten on deck without tables or chairs.

A *Early 19th century. When hammocks were used in the navy they were slung from the deck-head beams; they were stowed in the topgallant bulwark for protection against musket fire when not in use*

1 Hammocks slung under deck beams

2 Hammocks

stowed in bulwark

3 Mess table slung from overhead beam

4 Muzzle-loading gun with wooden carriage

B *Accommodation for 12 seamen in fo'c'sle on board a British three-masted iron bark of 900 tons, built in Glasgow, 1879*

1 Upper and lower bunks

2 Hawse pipes

3 Bowsprit

4 Cable compressors

5 Fore peak hatch

6 Windlass

7 Hatch to chain locker

8 Crew's lavatory with light house above

9 Fore hatch

C *Cabin accommodations on board a Swedish barkentine, built in Gävle, 1878*

1 Mizzenmast

2 Mess room

3 Mate's room

4 Second mate's and steward's room

5 Pantry

6 Cabin

7 Captain's bedroom

8 Alleyway

9 Sail locker and deck stores

10 Provisions

11 Entrance from deck

12 Steering compass

67

SOME TYPES OF LIFEBOAT

A   *Medieval ship towing her barge*
B   *Auxiliary coaster with her boat slung from short davits across her transom stern*
C   *Old pulling lifeboat*
D   *English sailing lifeboat, about 1900*
E   *Norwegian cruising lifeboat,* COLIN ARCHER. *1893*
F   *British self-righting lifeboat from 1960*
G   *Modern fiberglass lifeboat*

68

LANTERNS AND SIDELIGHTS

A   Swedish poop
    lantern from the
    18th century
B   Lantern with
    horn windows
    from the 18th
    century
C   Development of
    the poop lantern
1   1514, *Great Harry*
2   Middle of the
    16th century, Sir
    Francis Drake's
    Golden Hind
3   The 17th cen-
    tury. Dutch poop
    lantern
4   The 17th cen-
    tury. English
    poop lantern,
    Prince Royal
5   The 18th cen-
    tury, poop lan-
    tern of a big

French ship, built
at Brest in 1756
6   The 18th cen-
    tury, Swedish
    poop lantern
    (same as A)
D   *Riding light with
    a round wick
    lamp and Fresnel
    lens (A.J.
    Fresnel, French
    physicist, 1788–
    1827)*
E   *Sidelight for
    kerosene,
    paraffin oil, from
    the beginning of
    the 20th century*
F   *Starboard side
    light house on
    board big sailing
    ship, the 19th and
    20th centuries*

A

PUMPS

A   *Windmill pump
    with four sails,
    mounted on a
    turntable on top
    of a bipod erec-
    tion. The
    windmill pump
    always had rig-
    ging. The three-
    masted fore-and-
    aft schooner
    Eufrosine of
    Reval had a
    windmill pump
    forward of the
    foremast.*

1 Sails as seen from the side
2 Crankshaft
3 Turntable
4 Arm with braces, for setting the mill to the wind
5 The pump deck seating
6 Front view of windmill, showing two sails furled and two set
7 Three-masted fore-and-aft

schooner with a windmill pump

B *Old-type bilge pump, once common in small craft in the Baltic area. It was constructed from a piece of leather, which formed a bag, and gave good service.*

C *The standard bilge pump in small wooden sailing vessels. It was made from a straight tree trunk, bored through the heart.*
1 Trunk of pump
2 Pump bucket
3 Pump brake, handle

The SANTA MARIA *is shown once again to introduce the chapter on spars and rigging.*

74

SPARS AND RIGGING
By Sam Svensson

E xactly when and where primitive man first rigged a mast and sail to his simple boat remains a mystery. But quite early, he must have noticed that if he stood up in his craft, he would drift in the direction in which the wind was blowing. If he wanted to go in this direction, he might very well have speeded up his journey by holding up a cloak or animal hide to catch the wind. The time that elapsed between this first step and the introduction of the first real mast was certainly extremely long. And for many thousands of years, a single mast and a simple square sail were the limit of the ancient sailor's ability to rig a boat.

Far along through the ages, from the Old Empire in Egypt and well into the European Middle Ages, the single mast remained the only rig. One break in the monotony comes in the Roman era, when the Roman sailing ship had a bowsprit, sometimes seen as a greatly inclined foremast.

In Mediterranean lands, where the rowing galley played an important role, the mast and sail evolved somewhat differently than in Western Europe, where the single mast and square sail were prevalent up to the beginning of the 15th century. The standing rigging was very simple. Smaller ships at times had none, as in the rudimentary sailing boats of the early Scandinavian fishermen.

The running gear also was very simple. The halliard hoisting the sail was led aft and acted as a backstay, thus also serving to strengthen the mast when sailing. In the early Middle Ages bowlines were added to the sail and led forward to a spar, called the bowsprit, which was rigged out over the stem.

The shrouds were set up with deadeyes and lanyards, and the rigging was rattled down, forming rope ladders to facilitate going aloft. The Northern ship was also given a fighting top at the masthead. This top is actually very old. In fact, our oldest reproduction of the fighting top is to be found on an Egyptian relief from about 1200 B.C. The oldest top mentioned in Scandinavia is in the saga of Haakon Hardabred, 1159, contained in *Snorres Konungasagor.*

Sometime during the first half of the 15th century, larger ships were built with two or three masts. In Northwest Europe evolution quickly culminated in three masts. The mainmast kept its location in the middle of the ship, and from the beginning, the new masts were stepped in the fore- and aftercastles. It was most likely that flags or banners were first flown there, a common practice during the Crusades, and that it was just as easy to hoist a small sail on this same flagpole. One could even go so far as to say that every square sail, except the first, of course, was preceded by a flag on a pole. Thus, big ships unfurled a banner aloft on a staff in the fighting top, and toward the end of the 15th century, they appeared with a small sail on the same staff. From the beginning this small sail was handled by the men in the top, and it was from this that the name topsail was derived. The Dutch, Germans, and Scandinavians used a similar term; to them the sail was known as the "märssegel." The main topsail was soon followed by a second sail on the foremast. Both were small at first, but they continually increased in size as they came to be used more and more. The clews were sheeted to the yardarms below, and, with braces and clewlines leading down to the deck, the sail became more functional. As it could be set flatter, it could be used when sailing on the wind.

The triangular lateen sail, in general use in galleys and fishing boats of the Mediterranean, was eventually used as the mizzen in big ships all along the European coast. Its use had spread all the way to the Baltic Sea by the end of the Middle Ages. There, it gradually supplanted the older square sail as the mizzen. In the 250 years that followed, the lateen mizzen continued to be used in all larger ships.

The bowsprit had originally served only to lead the bowlines. By the end of the Middle Ages, however, a square sail had been rigged under the bowsprit. This sail was called a blind in Medieval English, as it wholly blocked the view ahead. It was, perhaps, the blind that prompted the need for a lookout aloft. Later, it became known as the spritsail.

By the last quarter of the 15th century, larger ships began to have as many as four masts. The two aftermost masts generally had lateen sails only, but the main mizzenmast could carry a triangular topsail on a topmast as well. The smaller mizzen,

SPARS OF A FOUR-MASTED BARK

1 Spike bowsprit
2 Fore lower mast
3 Fore yard
4 Fore top
5 Fore lower topsail yard
6 Fore topmast
7 Fore upper topsail yard, hoisted
8 Lifts
9 Fore topmast crosstree
10 Fore lower topgallant yard
11 Fore topgallant mast
12 Fore upper topgallant yard, hoisted
13 Fore royal mast in one with topgallant mast
14 Fore royal yard, hoisted
15 Fore royal pole
16 Main lower mast
17 Mainyard
18 Main top
19 Main lower topsail yard
20 Main topmast
21 Main upper topsail yard, hoisted
22 Main topmast crosstree
23 Main lower topgallant yard
24 Main topgallant mast
25 Main upper topgallant yard, hoisted

26	Main royal mast	35	Mizzen topmast crosstree	42	Jigger lower mast
27	Main royal yard, hoisted	36	Mizzen lower topgallant yard	43	Jigger top
28	Main royal pole	37	Mizzen topgallant mast	44	Jigger topmast
29	Mizzen lower mast	38	Mizzen upper topgallant yard, hoisted	45	Jigger pole
30	Crossjack yard			46	Spanker boom
31	Mizzen top			47	Lower spanker gaff
32	Mizzen lower topsail yard	39	Mizzen royal mast	48	Upper spanker gaff
33	Mizzen topmast	40	Mizzen royal yard, hoisted	49	Upper topsail halliard
34	Mizzen upper topsail yard, hoisted	41	Mizzen pole	50	Upper topgallant halliard
				51	Royal halliard

79

known as the bonaventure mizzen, usually reached abaft the ship where it was sheeted to a spar rigged out over the stern.

The topsail continued to grow in size, and around the middle of the 16th century, larger ships began to carry a third square sail, the topgallant sail, on the fore- and mainmasts. Until this time, however, the topmasts had been fixed extensions of the masts themselves and could not be rigged down. But around the 1570s, topmasts began to be stepped, to be fidded as the term was, so they could be rigged up or taken down depending on circumstances. This innovation, credited to the Dutch, was found to be very practical and was soon adopted for general use. Consequently, the fidded topmasts grew larger in relation to the lower masts; the topsail grew deeper, and the lower sail shallower.

Around 1620, it was common to equip the third mast with a square topsail. At the same time, the bonaventure mizzenmast was discarded. This marked the creation of the three-masted ship, with square sails on each mast. These early ships always had one yard less on the mizzenmast than on the fore- and mainmasts.

It was not until the latter half of the 18th century that rigging had evolved to the point where each mast had the same number of yards. This was the time when the term full-rigged ship became universal. The full-rigged ship usually referred to a merchant vessel, while sailing warships with such a rig were referred to by their rating: ship of the line, frigate, or sloop. The ships of the early 17th century were built with low heads and high sterns.

This design made them very hard to steer when the wind was abaft the beam, and the need for more headsail was keenly felt. To remedy the problem all larger ships of the 19th century were rigged with a spritsail topsail on a small mast at the end of the bowsprit. This sail was very impractical, though it was found to be very necessary, and it remained in use for over a hundred years before it was replaced with more practical and effective staysails.

Staysails had been used quite early in small craft, but not in the big ships. By the 1670s, however, the larger ships began carrying staysails, first between the masts and later over the bowsprit. This fore topmast staysail over the bowsprit was difficult to set because of the complicated rigging of the spritsail and sprit topsail. This was also the case with the staysails between the masts, because of the braces and bowlines leading to the stays. The staysails won out over the others, though, and in the beginning of the 18th century, the spritsail topmast was discarded and the running gear was gradually changed to make more room for the staysails of the mainmast. This development continued through the entire 18th century, and by the end of the century larger ships carried a staysail on every possible stay.

When the spritsail topmast was discarded in the first decade of the 18th century, a new spar, the jib boom, was rigged out on the bowsprit. A new staysail, called the jib, was placed over it ahead of the fore topmast staysail. After the middle of the same century, the lateen mizzen's long yard was exchanged for a gaff. This change occurred earlier in the smaller vessels than in the big ones.

During the Napoleonic wars, at the end of the century, other changes began to take place in the rigging. The mizzen was enlarged and sheeted to a boom extending over the stern. Under the bowsprit a new spar, called the martingale or dolphin striker, was inserted to improve the staying of the jib boom. This all developed into a new spar and staysail, the flying jib boom and flying jib, which were rigged outside the jib. A fourth yard above the topgallant yard, called the royal yard, now became more and more common on larger ships. Men-of-war always set it flying, while merchant ships set it as a standing sail carried on the upper part of the long topgallant mast. Only on hard winter trips was it rigged down. But this, of course, was true of all unnecessary rigging in prolonged bad weather.

The 19th century's mechanical revolution gradually began to influence the rigging of sailing ships. At first, it was merely a replacement on masts and yards of rope fittings, strops, and so on, with forged iron bands. Then the rope trusses of the lower yards were replaced with iron trusses, called patent trusses. Wherever possible, the heavier running rigging was replaced with chain, first the topsail ties and sheets and then the topgallant ties and sheets, and then just about anywhere chain

CLIPPER SHIPS

A   The Baltimore clipper is considered to be the forerunner of the clipper ship. After the 1812 war with Britain, certain American shipbuilders built fast vessels, schooners and brigs, which could engage in the most profitable of the world's trades. Mainly built in Virginia and Maryland, these small beamy craft were known throughout the world as Baltimore clippers. Rigged as a two-topsail schooner and carrying a great spread of canvas, this example, from 1820, had a very raked stem and maximum draft aft. She mounted four small cannons on each side.

B   FLYING CLOUD, 1851, build by Donald McKay at Boston, had single topsails, each with four reefs, topgallant sails with one reef, royals, and skysails. She had staysails on most stays and a whole set of studding sails, including the royals; she had studding-sail booms on the topgallant yards and jewel blocks for the royal studding sails on the royal yardarms.

C   NORMAN COURT, 1869, a British tea clipper, had four headsails, double topsails, topgallant sails, royals and a main skysail. All sails are clewed up to the bunt; she has two reefs in the topsails and a standing spanker gaff.

B

C

could be used to advantage. By the middle of the 19th century, British ships began to have the standing rigging replaced with wire. The rigging had previously been made of tarred hemp rope, but wire was cheaper and stronger and more durable. It had less surface exposed to the wind, and as the early attempts to build iron vessels were crowned with success, wire rigging was used more and more on larger ships, especially on steamships, which always had rigging and sails during the 19th century.

The huge topsails on larger sailing ships were extremely hard to handle during storms, when they had to be reefed. The American captain, Robert Forbes, devised a rig with double topsails in 1841. In 1854, another American sea captain, named Howes, improved this rig, and it became common in big ships. Twenty years later, in 1874, the largest ships were also rigged with double topgallant yards, as well as double topsail yards.

By this time, the use of wire for standing rigging and of chain for sheets and halliards was entirely accepted. Standing rigging now featured turnbuckles instead of deadeyes and lanyards, the system used ever since the early Middle Ages. Strong but stiff tarred hemp was replaced with Manila rope for running gear. Manila rope was softer and easier to work and just as strong, though not as durable as the hemp used formerly. Block sheaves were furnished with roller bearings, which also served to lighten the work on board ship. In fact, so much was done to ease the work on deck and aloft that the vessels could now be sailed with fewer hands, and larger ships could be sailed with the same crew as had been required for a smaller ship twenty years earlier. Sail handling became more mechanized in the large ships. In the 1890s, the Scottish sea captain, J.C.B. Jarvis, devised a geared mechanical winch that allowed a couple of men to brace the yards in the largest ships in rough weather. This was, of course, a big help. In the last of the big ships the topsail and topgallant halliards of chain were replaced with wire regulated by a hand-operated drum winch. Equipped with a conical drum, the winch considerably eased the effort of raising the yard.

All these innovations were part of that universal sequence of events that provided labor-saving devices in many areas of trade. For the sailing ship, these innovations had to be adapted to the special needs of the sea. They were needed to enable the sailing ship, with only the wind for power, to face up to the competition now provided by the coal- and oil-burning ships of the new age. It was obviously not a successful struggle, and the new means of propulsion became a prime factor in the disappearance of the sailing ship from all the seas of the world.

*Seven-masted fore-
and-aft schooner*
1 Foremast
2 Mainmast
3 Mizzenmast
4 Jiggermast
5 Driver mast
6 Pusher mast
7 Spanker mast

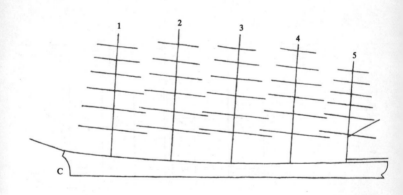

MASTS OF DIFFERENT SHIPS

A *Three-masted fullrigged ship*
1 Foremast
2 Mainmast
3 Mizzenmast

B *Four-masted fullrigged ship*
1 Foremast
2 Mainmast
3 Mizzenmast
4 Jiggermast

C *Five-masted fullrigged ship*
1 Foremast
2 Mainmast
3 Middlemast
4 Mizzenmast
5 Jiggermast

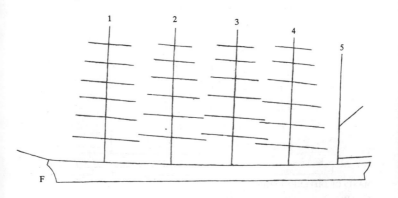

D	*Three-masted bark*	E	*Four-masted bark*	F	*Five-masted bark*
1	Foremast	1	Foremast	1	Foremast
2	Mainmast	2	Mainmast	2	Mainmast
3	Mizzenmast	3	Mizzenmast	3	Middlemast
		4	Jiggermast	4	Mizzenmast
				5	Jiggermast

MASTS OF DIFFERENT SHIPS

G *Brig*
1 Foremast
2 Mainmast

H *Brigantine*
1 Foremast
2 Mainmast

I *Three-masted barkentine*
1 Foremast

2 Mainmast
3 Mizzenmast

J *Ketch*
1 Mainmast
2 Mizzenmast

K *Six-masted barkentine*
1 Foremast
2 Mainmast

3 Mizzenmast
4 Jiggermast
5 Driver mast
6 Spanker mast

L *Two-masted fore- and- aft schooner*
1 Foremast
2 Mainmast

88

M *Three-masted fore-and-aft schooner*
1 Foremast
2 Mainmast
3 Mizzenmast

N *Four-masted fore-and-aft schooner*
1 Foremast
2 Mainmast
3 Mizzenmast
4 Spanker mast

O *Six-masted fore-and-aft schooner*
1 Foremast
2 Mainmast
3 Mizzenmast
4 Jiggermast
5 Driver mast
6 Spanker mast

P *Five-masted fore-and-aft schooner*
1 Foremast
2 Mainmast
3 Mizzenmast
4 Jiggermast
5 Spanker mast

MASTS AND SPARS IN DIFFERENT SHIPS

A *Yawl*
B *Sloop, about 1900*
C *Ketch, end of the 19th century*
D *Topsail schooner*
E *Barkentine*
1 Mast coat
2 Truck
3 Foremast
4 Mainmast
5 Snow mast
8 Mizzenmast
9 Laeisz mast
10 Lower mast

11 Fore-and-aft-rigged topmast
12 Square-rigged topmast
13 Topgallant mast
14 Royal mast
15 Skysail mast
16 Moonsail mast
17 Fore yard
18 Main yard

19 Crossjack yard
20 Topsail yard for single topsail
21 Lower topsail yard
22 Upper topsail yard
23 Topgallant yard for single topgallant sail

24 Lower topgallant yard
25 Upper topgallant yard
26 Royal yard
27 Skysail yard
28 Moonsail yard
29 Masthead and housing of top-mast

The terminology for masts varies in different languages. Numbers 6 and 7, missing in list above, refer to Teutonic languages only.

F

MASTS AND SPARS IN DIFFERENT SHIPS

F *Three-masted
   fore-and-aft
   schooner*
G *American five-
   masted fore-and-
   aft schooner*
 1 Mast coat
 2 Truck
 3 Foremast
 4 Mainmast
 5 Snow mast
 8 Mizzenmast
 9 Laeisz mast
10 Lower mast
11 Fore-and-aft-
    rigged topmast
12 Square-rigged
    topmast
13 Topgallant mast
14 Royal mast
15 Skysail mast
16 Moonsail mast
17 Fore yard
18 Main yard
19 Crossjack yard
20 Topsail yard for
    single topsail
21 Lower topsail
    yard
22 Upper topsail
    yard
23 Topgallant yard
    for single
    topgallant sail
24 Lower topgallant
    yard
25 Upper topgallant
    yard
26 Royal yard
27 Skysail yard
28 Moonsail yard

29 Masthead and
    housing of top-
    mast
30 Jiggermast
31 Spankermast

93

H *Snow with single topsails*
I *Three-masted bark with double topsails*
J *Four-masted bark with short topgallant masts abaft the top-masts*

J

1 Mast coat
2 Truck
3 Foremast
4 Mainmast
5 Snow mast
8 Mizzenmast
9 Laeisz mast
10 Lower mast
11 Fore-and-aft-
   rigged topmast
12 Square-rigged
   topmast
13 Topgallant mast
14 Royal mast
15 Skysail mast
16 Moonsail mast
17 Fore yard
18 Main yard
19 Crossjack yard
20 Topsail yard for
   single topsail
21 Lower topsail
   yard
22 Upper topsail
   yard
23 Topgallant yard
   for single
   topgallant sail
24 Lower topgallant
   yard
25 Upper topgallant
   yard
26 Royal yard
27 Skysail yard
28 Moonsail yard
29 Masthead and
   housing of top-
   mast
30 Jiggermast

95

MASTS AND SPARS IN DIFFERENT SHIPS

K *Four-masted bark with royals and double topgallant sails, skysails on the main and the mizzen*

L *Three-masted, full-rigged ship, American clipper, about 1850, with skysails and a main moonsail*

M *Ship, about 1700*

1 Mast coat
2 Truck
3 Foremast
4 Mainmast
5 Snow mast
8 Mizzenmast
9 Laeisz mast
10 Lower mast
11 Fore-and-aft-rigged topmast
12 Square-rigged topmast
13 Topgallant mast
14 Royal mast
15 Skysail mast
16 Moonsail mast
17 Fore yard
18 Main yard
19 Crossjack yard
20 Topsail yard for single topsail
21 Lower topsail yard
22 Upper topsail yard
23 Topgallant yard for single topgallant sail
24 Lower topgallant yard
25 Upper topgallant yard
26 Royal yard
27 Skysail yard
28 Moonsail yard
29 Masthead and housing of topmast
30 Jiggermast
31 Spankermast
32 Flagpole

97

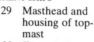

MASTS AND SPARS IN DIFFERENT SHIPS

N	Five-masted full-rigged ship (Preussen, the only ship of this rig ever built)	29	Masthead and housing of top-mast
1	Mast coat	30	Jiggermast
2	Truck	31	Spankermast
3	Foremast	32	Flagpole
4	Mainmast	33	Laeisz yard
5	Snow mast	34	Jigger yard
8	Mizzenmast		
9	Laeisz mast		
10	Lower mast		
11	Fore-and-aft-rigged topmast		
12	Square-rigged topmast		
13	Topgallant mast		
14	Royal mast		
15	Skysail mast		
16	Moonsail mast		
17	Fore yard		
18	Main yard		
19	Crossjack yard		
20	Topsail yard for single topsail		
21	Lower topsail yard		
22	Upper topsail yard		
23	Topgallant yard for single topgallant sail		
24	Lower topgallant yard		
25	Upper topgallant yard		
26	Royal yard		
27	Skysail yard		
28	Moonsail yard		

MASTS AND TOPS

A *Mast from the end of the 17th century (from an old book on ship building)*
1 Mast step in keelson
2 Lower mast
3 Cheeks
4 Trestletrees supporting rigging and topmast
5 Lower cap
6 Topmast
7 Topmast crosstree
8 Topmast cap, or Dutch cap, made in one piece; *a:* as seen from the side; *b:* another cap made in two pieces as seen from below; *c:* the same as seen from above
9 Topgallant mast
10 Topgallant crosstree
11 Topgallant cap
12 Flagpole
13 Truck

B	*Early medieval top*
C	*Medieval top*
D	*Medieval top*
E	*Top, about 1550*
F	*Top in the 17th century*
G	*Top in the 18th century*
H	*Top in the 19th century*

I	*Lower mast seen from port side*
1	Lower masthead
2	Trestletrees
3	Cheeks
4	Rope wooldings around the mast
5	Heel of mast

101

STANDING RIGGING OF A FOUR-MASTED BARK

A *Jigger mast* (identical with mizzenmast of a three-masted bark)
1 Jigger lower mast
2 Jigger topmast
3 Jigger topgallant mast
4 Jigger topgallant stay
5 Jigger topmast stay

6 Jigger topmast rigging or shrouds
7 Jigger stay
8 Jigger rigging or jigger shrouds
B *Foremast* (identical with mainmast and mizzenmast except in the lead of the stays)

1 Fore lower mast
2 Fore topmast
3 Fore topgallant mast
4 Fore royal mast
5 Fore royal stay
6 Fore topgallant stay
7 Outer jib stay
8 Inner jib stay
9 Fore topmast stay
10 Fore stay

11	Fore rigging or shrouds	
12	Fore cap backstays	
13	Fore topmast backstays	
14	Fore topmast rigging or shrouds	
15	Fore topmast cap backstay	
16	Fore topgallant backstays	
17	Fore royal backstay	
18	Fore topgallant rigging or shrouds	
19	Main royal stay	
20	Main topgallant stay	
21	Main topmast stay	
22	Main stay	
23	Bob stay	
24	Outer bob stay	

103

STAYS AND SHROUDS

A *Square-rigged
    foremast of a big
    modern sailing
    ship as seen from
    aft, with the sails
    furled on the port
    side (I) and set
    on the starboard
    side (II)*
1 Lower rigging or
   shrouds
2 Cap backstay
3 Futtock rigging,
   futtock shrouds
4 Royal back stay
5 Topgallant
   backstay(s)
6 Topmast cap
   backstay
7 Topmast
   backstay(s)
8 Topmast rigging,
   topmast shrouds
9 Topmast futtock
   rigging
10 Topgallant rig-
   ging, topgallant
   shrouds
B *This picture of a
    top, seen from
    the side, shows
    how shrouds and
    stays are fastened
    to the mast*

DIFFERENT PARRELS

A *Parrel with cleats on a wooden yard*
1 Topmast
2 Yard
3 Wooden cleats
4 Half-iron hoop served with leather
5 Pins forming hinges to open the parrel
6 Iron band to take the tie
7 Iron straps and bolts securing parrel to yard

B *Tub parrel for iron yard*
1 Topmast
2 Yard
3 Tub divided in halves
4 Iron binding for same
5 Gooseneck bolt
6 Iron bands to take parrel and tie
7 Yoke for the parrel
8 Yoke for the tie
9 Eye bolt for quarterblock

C *Parrel, sliding on T-bar in a big ship*
1 Topmast
2 Topsail yard
3 T-bar
4 Slide
5 Two-way coupling
6 Tie
7 Connecting chain keeping slide in place
8 Eye bolts for quarterblocks

TOP AND CROSSTREES

Details around the top
1 Topmast, built in one with lower mast
2 Lower topsail yard with its truss
3 Lower topsail yard tie
4 Lower cap backstays
5 Quarter block for upper topsail sheet and topsail clewline
6 Topmast rigging, ratlines not shown
7 Futtock shrouds
8 Top
9 Fairleader
10 Running gear rove through fairleader
11 Lower yard with its truss

12 Lower yard tie
13 Lower stay, doubled
14 Lower rigging, ratlines not shown
15 Pendants for braces from mast ahead, leading to brace winch
16 Quarterblock for topsail sheet and the course clewgarnet
17 Buntline with its leading blocks

TOPGALLANT CROSSTREES

Details around the
topgallant crosstrees
1 Topmast
2 Topgallant mast
3 Topmast head
4 Topgallant
   crosstrees
5 Spreader of
   topgallant
   backstays
6 Topmast cap
7 Lower topgallant
   yard
8 Lower topgallant
   truss
9 Lower topgallant
   tie
10 Upper topsail
   yard
11 Upper topsail
   parrel, slide run-
   ning on a T-bar
12 Topsail halliard,
   wire tackle lead-
   ing to winch on
   deck
13 Leading block
   for topsail brace
   from mast ahead
14 Topmast
   backstays
15 Topmast cap
   backstay
16 Topgallant fut-
   tock shrouds
17 Topmast stay
18 Topgallant rig-
   ging
19 Spreader lift
20 Quarterblock for
   lower topgallant
   clewline and up-
   per topgallant
   sheet
21 Quarterblock for
   topsail downhaul
   and lower
   topgallant sheet

LOWER PART OF RIGGING, PORT SIDE

1 Shrouds, lower ends of which are served with spun yarn
2 Upper deadeye
3 Deadeye turned in cutter-stay fashion
4 Lowerdeadeye in iron strap
5 Chain plate
6 Lanyard, standing part with wall knot
7 Hauling end of lanyard hitched
8 Ratlines in rigging
9 Seizing of ratline to shroud
10 Wooden batten secured to shroud with seizing wire

BOWSPRITS

The bowsprit and its rigging at the end of the 16th century

1 Foremast
2 Bowsprit
3 Spritsail yard
4 Jackstaff
5 Foreyard
6 Foresail with bonnet
7 Fore topsail
8 Spritsail
9 Gammoning
10 Forestay lanyard
11 Fore topmast stay
12 Fore topgallant stay
13 Fore sheet
14 Fore tack
15 Spritsail sheet
16 Spritsail clewline
17 Spritsail braces
18 Spritsail lifts
19 Fore topsail bowline
20 Fore topgallant bowline

BOWSPRIT OF A FRIGATE, 1890

1	Bowsprit
2	Tenon for bowsprit cap
3	Bowsprit cap
4	Bowsprit bees
5	Jib boom
6	Heel of flying jib boom
7	Martingale boom or dolphin striker
8	Whisker
9	Inner and outer bobstays
10	Bowsprit shrouds
11	Forestay
12	Preventer forestay
13	Fore topmast stay
14	Fore topmast preventer stay
15	Jib stay
16	Jib outhaul
17	Jib boom guy
18	Flying jib boom guy
19	Martingale stay
20	Backropes or martingale guys
21	Flying jib stay
22	Fore topgallant stay
23	Fore royal stay
24	Jib boom horse, footrope
25	Gaskets
26	Fore topsail bowline
27	Whisker lift
28	Fore topmast staysail tack
29	Jib boom gammoning
30	Jib boom heel stay
31	Lanyards for stays
32	Iron fitting for whiskers

111

SEIZINGS AND RIGGING SCREWS

A *Three stages of making an old-fashioned round seizing; formerly used on hemp shrouds*

B 1 Shroud or backstay of wire served over with spun yarn
2 Rigging seizings of galvanized wire
3 Solid heart thimble with a hole for the sheer pole
4 Upper end of rigging screw

C *Details from lower part of rigging, port side.*
1 Surplus end of lanyard, made up
2 Lower deadeye in iron strap
3 Upper deadeye
4 Hauling end of lanyard, hitched
5 Wall knot
6 Double wall knot

D 1 Lower ends of four port side shrouds
2 Rigging seizings
3 Sheer Pole
4 Rigging screws or turnbuckles
5 Upper ends of chain plates

BOWSPRIT

A *Bowsprit with jib boom and rigging, end of the 18th century*
1 Bowsprit
2 Jib boom
3 Flying jib boom
4 Spritsail yard
5 Foreyard
6 Studdingsail boom
7 Fore tack bumpkin
8 Bobstay
9 Forestay
10 Fore topmast stay
11 Jibstay
12 Fore topgallant stay
13 Flying jibstay
14 Royal stay
15 Jib boom guy
16 Flying jib boom guy
17 Spritsail braces
18 Fore topmast staysail downhaul
19 Weather side jib sheet
20 Weather side flying jib sheet

B **Bowsprit with spritsail topmast and rigging, from the 17th century**

1	Foremast
2	Bowsprit
3	Spritsail yard
4	Spritsail topmast
5	Spritsail topsail yard
6	Fore rigging
7	Gammoning
8	Forestay
9	Fore topmast stay
10	Fore topgallant stay
11	Spritsail topmast backstay
12	Fore sheet
13	Fore tack
14	Fore clewgarnet
15	Fore bowline
16	Spritsail sheet
17	Spritsail clewline
18	Spritsail braces
19	Fore topsail bowline
20	Fore topgallant bowline
21	Spritsail topsail sheet
22	Spritsail topsail clewline
23	Spritsail topsail braces
24	Spritsail topsail lift

BOWSPRIT OF THE SHIP, PRINCE OSCAR, BUILT IN 1864

1 Shark's tail	8 Outer jib stay	15 Inner jib
2 Fore royal stay	9 Outer jib tack	16 Flying jib boom guy
3 Fore topgallant stay	10 Outer jib downhaul	17 Outer jib boom guy
4 Flying jib tack	11 Outer jib	
5 Flying jib downhaul	12 Inner jib stay	18 Inner jib boom guy
6 Flying jib	13 Inner jib tack	19 Bowsprit cap
7 Flying jib boom	14 Inner jib downhaul	20 Swinging boom,

fore guy lead
block
21 Jib boom
22 Bowsprit
23 Fore topmast stay
24 Fore topmast
    staysail tack
25 Fore topmast
    staysail downhaul
26 Fore topmast
    staysail
27 Fore stay
28 Pinrail for
    staysails'

downhauls
29 Whisker boom
30 Flying jib sheet
31 Outer jib sheet
32 Inner jib sheet
33 Fore topmast
    staysail sheet
34 Pinrail
35 Bowsprit shroud
36 Martingale
    backrope (Mar-
    tingale guy)
37 Bobstay
38 Martingale or

Dolphin striker
39 Inner martingale
    (stay)
40 Middle mar-
    tingale (stay)
41 Outer martingale
    (stay)
42 Foot rope
43 Bitts
44 Capstan working
    the windlass
45 Cathead

117

DETAILS OF MAINMAST AND MAINYARD OF A SNOW, ABOUT 1800

1	Mainmast	17	Mainyard stirrups
2	Mainyard	18	Main clewgarnet
3	Main top	19	Reef tackle
4	Trysail mast	20	Reef earing
5	Trysail gaff	21	Topsail sheet
6	Main rigging or shrouds	22	Topsail clewline
7	Futtock shrouds	23	Topsail bowline bridle
8	Topmast shrouds	24	Fore topsail brace
9	Mainstay	25	Trysail brails
10	Mainsail		
11	Main topsail		
12	Trysail		
13	Mainyard sling		
14	Main lift		
15	Main brace		
16	Mainyard footrope		

DETAILS OF MAINMAST HEAD, SHIP OF THE LINE, 1750

1 Mainmast	17 Main footrope
2 Trestle trees	18 Main clewgarnet
3 Maintop	19 Main topsail sheet
4 Lower masthead	20 Main jeers
5 Heel of topmast	
6 Main cap	
7 Mainyard	
8 Main parrel	
9 Parrel tackle	
10 Main rigging or shrouds	
11 Mainstay	
12 Spring stay	
13 Futtock shrouds	
14 Topmast shrouds	
15 Mizzen topmast stay	
16 Main lift	

119

RIGGING OF OLDER STEAMERS

A, B	H Main gaff topsail	9 Fore yard
Steamer from about 1890, rigged as a three-masted topsail schooner	I Mizzen staysail	10 Topsail yard
	J Mizzen	11 Topgallant yard
	K Mizzen gaff topsail	12 Fore boom
A Fore topmast staysail	1 Foremast	13 Fore gaff
	2 Mainmast	14 Main boom
B Fore staysail	3 Mizzenmast	15 Main gaff
C Foresail; Boom foresail	4 Fore topmast	16 Mizzen boom
	5 Fore topgallant mast	17 Mizzen gaff
D Topsail	6 Main topmast	18 Fore topmast stay
E Topgallant sail	7 Main topgallant mast	19 Fore stay
F Main staysail	8 Mizzen topmast	20 Main stay
G Mainsail		21 Main topmast stay

22	Main topgallant stay	32	Main vang		*the possibility of reefing without a man leaving the deck*
23	Mizzen stay	33	Mizzen vang		
24	Mizzen topmast stay	34	Boom foresail sheet	1	Foresail
25	Fore braces	35	Main sheet	2	Topsail with Collin's and Pinkney's Patent (3)
26	Topsail braces	36	Mizzen sheet		
27	Topgallant braces	37	Flagstaff		
28	Fore boom topping lift	38	Pole compass	4	Topgallant sail
29	Main boom topping lift	39	Ventilator	5	Bermuda-type trysail traveling on a bar abaft the mast
30	Mizzen boom topping lift	40	Anchor davit		
31	Fore vang	C	*Patent reefing topsails were not unusual in the old steamers carrying sails, because of*		

*Opposite is a 1492
nao; it is Columbus'
SANTA MARIA and
it introduces the sec-
tion about sails. The
color in the picture
illustrates the fact that
the chapter deals with
flags as well.*

THE SAIL
By Sam Svensson

The oldest sail we know is the square sail. For many thousands of years no other types were used. The distinguishing feature of the square sail is that the same side is always turned to the wind. This is a simple, fundamental principle, and none of the aerodynamic inventions of recent years have changed the square sail or influenced its value for sailing on the high seas.

The fore-and-aft sail, which can face into the wind with either side, is a more recent development. What aerodynamics could not do for the square sail it has succeeded in doing for the fore-and-aft sail. The latter is very effective in close-hauled sailing and is superior for use while cruising. Today, it is the sail most used for sport sailing among off-shore islands where winds are variable and the water is smooth. Because the fore-and-aft sail always has its forward bolt rope as the windward edge and the leech as the leeward edge, it can be cut with a favorable curvature. The square sail, on the other hand, has the starboard or port leech alternately as the windward edge, resulting in a different curvature. The value of the modern fore-and-aft sail on the wind is, however, outweighed by the advantages of the more secure square sail in running before the wind in stormy and high seas. Almost all sailing on the high seas has been done with the square sail. The oldest known reproduction of a boat equipped with a sail is painted on an Egyptian clay urn from the predynastic period. Estimated to be from about 4000 B.C., it could actually be even older. Furthermore, the evidence is not conclusive that this painting shows the world's first sail. Past cultures of which we have no knowledge may very well have had sailing vessels thousands of years before.

Contemporary writings and pictures prove that the sailors of ancient lands in the eastern Mediterranean used sails. In the twenty-seventh chapter of Ezekiel, the ships of Tyrus are described as having cedar masts from Lebanon, gay, embroidered sails of fine Egyptian linen, and awnings of blue and purple cloth from the Isles of Elisha. The decoration of the sails indicates that they were used both for propulsion and as a means of identification.

We have no record of when the art of sailing was brought to Scandinavia, but by the Viking Age it was certainly hundreds, perhaps even thousands, of years old. Early Nordic sails were made of homespun wool and lacked the durability of linen sails. The cloth would stretch under the force of the wind, and the large sail would sag more and more until it burst. To strengthen the sail and hold it more evenly, a supporting net was fastened to the forward side. The net, often of a different color than the sail, was either of rope, of cloth bands, or of interwoven sennit. The foot of the sail was held down by a number of sheets, forming bridles, all to hold the sail flatter. By the Viking Age, linen sails were in use on larger ships. These sails could be set flatter, making for better sailing on the wind. The long journeys made by the Vikings in European waters and over the Atlantic Ocean would have been impossible if their ships had not been able to sail in all kinds of wind. At the dawn of Swedish history, the cruising ability of the ships of the time is illustrated in the saga of the King of the Sveas, Erik Väderhatt, who, according to history, could turn the wind so that he never had a headwind.

The majority of ships continued to have only one mast and a single sail for many years. Only after the later Middle Ages did larger ships commonly appear with two or three masts and sails – one sail on each mast. By the end of the 15th century, however, a new sail was set at the head of the mainmast. It was originally very small and was handled by the men in the top (an early masthead castle). It derived its name, the topsail, from this position. Another sail was added under the bowsprit; this was called the spritsail or blind, as it blocked the view ahead. Eventually, a topsail was also added to the foremast. By the middle of the 16th century, then, a large three-masted ship carried six sails: the spritsail under the bowsprit, two sails on the foremast, two sails on the mainmast, and one sail on the mizzenmast. The sail on the mizzenmast was always a triangular lateen sail at this time.

The origin of the lateen sail is unknown. At the fall of the Roman Empire in 476 A.D., all ships had square sails. After that, sources of information on ships and navigation in the Mediterranean are not available for several hundreds of years. Not until the end of the 9th century do Greek manuscripts show some miniatures of ships with triangular sails under an inclined yard. Even today these sails are called lateen sails. These were probably introduced into the Mediterranean by the Arabs, but

125

DIFFERENT SAILS

1 Spritsails
2 Standing lug sail
3 Square sail
4 Gaff sail
5 Bermuda sail
6 Gunter rig
7 Lateen sails
8 Staysail rig

no one knows whether their origin is Arabian or Polynesian. Up to the 13th century, the lateen sail was in use exclusively along the Mediterranean. But from that time on, the square sail began to make a comeback under western European impetus. The lateen sail was used, at this time, along the whole European coastline, especially as a mizzen on larger ships. It probably reached the Baltic by the latter half of the 15th century, about the same time as the carvel or smooth-sided shipbuilding technique came along. Down to the middle of the 18th century, the lateen sail was in general international use as the mizzen. It was then replaced by the gaff mizzen. The coastal galleys of the Swedish navy continued to employ lateen sails as long as these ships were in use, the last one being built in 1749. But the development of sail went in the opposite direction as regards sails on small barges and boats, and in the Mediterranean, the Red Sea, and the Persian Gulf the lateen sail can be seen on these craft even today.

As the lateen sail has to be set on the leeward side of the mast, it is not suitable for tacking with short boards in a narrow channel. The rule is that lateen-rigged craft wear, with the sail being taken around forward of the mast and sheeted on the new lee side. Large Arab dhows still sail in this same manner from the Persian Gulf to East African ports, as far down as Zanzibar. They never beat against the wind but run to Africa in the favorable wind of the northeast monsoon and return with the southwest monsoon to the Persian Gulf. They are, therefore, limited to only one such round trip a year, the same as the Indian grain carriers that make only one voyage a year to Rangoon to pick up rice for Ceylon.

The lateen sail was the world's first fore-and-aft sail. While it enjoyed great popularity in the Near East and Mediterranean for a long time, other types of sail began to appear in Europe. We can follow this development especially well in Holland and Friesland.

During the 16th century, Holland became the world's most powerful maritime nation, replacing the sea power of the Hanseatic League. Using the rich Rhineland inland waterways, the Dutch had developed navigation with small ships in canals and rivers and in the shallow coastal waters between the islands.

The inability to beat and especially to tack in a narrow channel, when using a square sail, created the need for new types of sail, and Dutch art records two new fore-and-aft sails, the spritsail and the staysail. The former was a simple rectangular sail with one side laced to the mast and extended by a diagonally placed sprit. The sail was found to be very practical, and, as a result, it became the most commonly used sail in small sailing boats of Northern Europe. It was eventually used in larger craft as well and is now best known on the Thames River barges, which still use it today.

With the spritsail set abaft the mast, there was an empty space under the stay on the forward side of the mast, and it was only natural to set a triangular sail on that stay. By the middle of the first half of the 16th century, boats with a spritsail and fore staysail were in use in Holland. The development of the fore staysail was followed by a new staysail called the jib, which was set on a jib boom outside the stem. These staysails were soon in general use in small vessels in Western Europe, but it was not until the end of the 17th century that staysails appeared on the larger, square-sailed ships.

Another fore-and-aft sail, the lug sail, came to Europe somewhat later. The lug sail was a rectangular one that was hoisted with an inclined yard, with the halliard nearer the forward yardarm. Again there is evidence that the lug sail was known in the eastern Mediterranean about 100 A.D.

We are not sure whether the lug sail evolved from the lateen sail by cutting away the forward section or whether it came from the square sail by moving the halliard nearer one end of the yard and at the same time shifting the sail's tack amidships. The lug sail was used mostly in Western Europe, in the English and French waters of the English Channel. French fishermen and smugglers, as well as privateers and customs boats with sharp lines and fast hulls, were often rigged with lug sails; the type was sometimes called the *Chasse Marée*. English and Scottish fishermen in the North Sea also employed the lug sail, until they gave up the use of sails. Sailing ship's boats, both in the merchant marine and the navy, generally had lug sails as well, most often in one-masted, but also in two- or three-masted, rigs.

SAILS OF A FOUR-MASTED BARK

(HERZOGIN CECILIE)
This four-masted bark was built in 1902 by Rickmers shipyard at Bremerhaven for the Norddeutscher Lloyd at Bremen. It was a big sailing vessel of 3,242 gross tons or 4,350 dw. She was a good sailer and made many excellent voyages. During World War I, she was interned at Coquimbo, Chile.

After the war, she brought a cargo of nitrate to Ostend and was there allocated to the French government. In November, 1921, she was purchased by Gustaf Erikson, Mariehamn, and under his flag was employed chiefly in the Australian grain trade. She foundered on April 25, 1936, off Salcombe, Devon-

shire, after running aground in heavy fog.

1 Flying jib
2 Outer jib
3 Inner jib
4 Fore topmast staysail
5 Fore sail, fore course
6 Fore lower topsail
7 Fore upper topsail
8 Fore lower topgallant sail

130

9	Fore upper topgallant sail	17	Main lower topgallant sail	25	Mizzen upper topsail
10	Fore royal	18	Main upper topgallant sail	26	Mizzen lower topgallant sail
11	Main topmast staysail	19	Main royal	27	Mizzen upper topgallant sail
12	Main topgallant staysail	20	Mizzen topmast staysail	28	Mizzen royal
13	Main royal staysail	21	Mizzen topgallant staysail	29	Jigger staysail
14	Main sail, main course	22	Mizzen royal staysail sail	30	Jigger topmast staysail
15	Main lower topsail	23	Crossjack, mizzen course	31	Jigger topgallant staysail
16	Main upper topsail	24	Mizzen lower topsail	32	Lower spanker
				33	Upper spanker
				34	Gaff topsail

131

There were two types of lug sails: the standing and the dipping. The tack of the dipping lug was made fast a little before the mast, near the stem. It was always set to the lee of the mast and had to be shifted to the new leeward side at every tack. A standing lug had the tack at the mast and could take the wind from either side, though it was most effective when the yard was on the lee side of the mast. In ancient times, it was very common for the masts of fishing boats to have no shrouds, and one sailed only "on the wood," as it was called. The sail was set on the lee side of the mast, with the halliards leading to the weather quarter and serving as a backstay to sail on. Coming about, the sail was shifted to the new lee and the halliard to the new weather side.

In addition to the fore-and-aft sail on fishing boats and smaller vessels, the lateen sail in the Mediterranean, the lug sail in Western Europe, and the spritsail in Northern Europe, there were many small craft that still used square sails. The "Roslagen" sloops from Stockholm's archipelago used square sails until the end of the 18th century, as did the Norwegian "Nordland" yachts for as long as they used sails.

The original square sail, which had served maritime navigation for several thousands of years, was entirely different from the various kinds of fore-and-aft sails. When ships became larger and masts taller, the number of sails on each mast also increased. After the middle of the 16th century, the larger ships set a third sail, the topgallant sail, which was rigged above the topsail. In the beginning of the 16th century the larger ships set a third sail, the topgallant sail, which was rigged above the topsail. An impractical square sail, its mast was very badly stayed and often prone to damage. It remained in use on larger ships, however, for more than a hundred years, before it was replaced by a more practical staysail, the jib.

The first staysails on larger ships were set between the masts as the main staysail, the main topmast staysail, and the mizzen staysail. In addition, there was the fore topmast staysail, which was placed on a special stay from the fore topmast head and parallel with the fore topmast stay. This stay was actually so cluttered with blocks and running gear for the spritsail that the additional rigging for the new staysail caused many difficulties.

The fore topmast staysail was, however, a more effective head-sail than either of the square sails on the bowsprit, and at the beginning of the 18th century, the spritsail topsail disappeared. It was replaced, as was said earlier, by a new staysail called the jib. This was set on a new spar, the jib boom, which was rigged on the extension of the bowsprit.

By the beginning of the 18th century, rigging became more functional. The sails could be reefed effectively, and the rigging allowed for better bracing, which meant better sailing to wind-ward. The studding sail, which on occasion was already used in the previous century, became more common. It was used, when running free, to increase the sail area, much as the modern spinnaker functions on sailing yachts.

Toward the end of the 18th century, larger ships began to use a fourth square sail above the topgallant sail. It was called the royal. In men-of-war it was always set flying, *i.e.,* it was set from the deck, and when furled, it was taken down on deck. But in merchant ships it became a standing sail with the royal yard left aloft.

An important improvement in types of sail was made at the beginning of the 19th century, as the jackstay on the yards came into use. The head of the sail was bent to the jackstay on the forward upper side of the yard instead of having lashings around the yard. This made the work easier when bending and unbend-ing sail, and especially when furling sail. The sail could then be rolled up on top of the yards, where it could be easily secured under the gaskets. Without the jackstay on the yards, the larger steel ships of a later period could not have sailed with the small crews they had.

After the Napoleonic era, larger ships were rigged with a fifth sail, the skysail, which was carried over the royal. It was never widely used but was seen mostly at the time of the clipper ships, in the middle of the century. Some clippers carried still another sail, the moonsail, usually set only on the mainmast. Exaggera-tions could always be found, and one of the most unusual occurs in a story of the English corvette hunting for slavers in the steaming heat and calm waters of the Bay of Benin. Seamen tell of it carrying a royal, skysail, moonsail, heaven poker, angel poker, and cloud disturber — all over the topgallant sail.

SAILS IN VARIOUS SAILING VESSELS

A *Four-masted fore-
  and-aft schooner*
1 Flying jib
2 Outer jib
3 Inner jib
4 Fore staysail
5 Square foresail
6 Raffee
7 Foresail
8 Fore gaff topsail
9 Mainsail
10 Main gaff topsail
11 Mizzen

12 Mizzen gaff
   topsail
13 Jigger or spanker
14 Jigger gaff topsail

B *Brig*
1 Flying jib
2 Jib
3 Fore topmast
   staysail
4 Foresail
5 Fore lower
   topsail
6 Fore upper
   topsail
7 Fore topgallant
   sail
8 Fore royal

9	Mainsail	**C**	*Two-topsail schooner*
10	Main lower topsail	1	Flying jib
11	Main upper topsail	2	Outer jib
12	Main topgallant sail	3	Inner jib
13	Main royal	4	Fore staysail
14	Trysail	5	Foresail
		6	Fore topsail
		7	Fore topgallant sail
		8	Mainsail
		9	Main topsail
		10	Main topgallant sail

D *Three-masted staysail schooner*

1 Flying jib
2 Jib
3 Fore staysail
4 Fore trysail
5 Main staysail
6 Main trysail
7 Mizzen staysail
8 Jib-headed spanker

Expanding 19th-century industry gave rigging a more delicate look. Mechanical improvements in the rigging also influenced the sails. Thimbles and clasp hooks were introduced, and, later, shackles. Both square-sail halliards and sheets were made of chain. Previously, the clews of square sails had been part of the bolt rope, which formed an eye in which the sheet and clewline were fastened. It now became common to put a thimble in the clew, and later to lead a cringle from the eye. Still later, a wrought-iron clew was spliced into the bolt ropes. In larger ships, with double topsail sheets, the clew was formed by a stropped block through which the sheet was reeved. The sheet was still made of hemp. In navy ships, where working the sails quickly became more and more important, all running gear was equipped with toggles, so that bowlines, buntlines, clewlines, and sheets could be let go in just a few seconds and a topsail shifted in just a few minutes.

When large ships began to be built of iron and then of steel, during the last half of the century, the standing rigging, and then the running gear, was made of wire. The sails were also influenced. The huge square sails were given both leech and foot ropes of wire, and a bolt rope of wire could be used for foot and leech on the staysail but not for the luff, as this had to be folded along the stay when the sail was hauled down.

In addition to the fore-and-aft sails already mentioned – the lateen sail, spritsail, staysail, and lug sail – there is yet another, the gaff sail, that gradually came to dominate all the others. It evolved from the spritsail by means of shortening the sprit, raising it, and fastening it to the sail's head. To keep it in place, with the forward end against the mast, the end was shaped as a throat or gaff with a branch fork, which partly covered the mast and gave both the spar and the sail its name, the gaff. To be able to hoist the gaff sail the mast had to be made higher than the sail, so that the gaff's halliards, the inner throat halliard, and the outer peak halliard could be fastened above the gaff.

Pictures of the gaff sail appear later than those of the spritsail but go as far back as the middle of the 17th century. Slowly, the gaff sail won out over the other fore-and-aft sails. Mail packets and other semi-official craft which sailed with mail and passengers between specified ports, revenue cutters, the larger pilot boats, and similar craft were among the first to use the gaff sail. During the 18th century, smaller merchant ships and warships began more often to be rigged with the gaff sail. Various types of early schooners and sloops all had gaff sails.

During the 19th century, larger merchant ships, for example the three-masted fore-and-aft schooners and barkentines, began to employ the gaff rig. Particularly in North America, by the end of the century, multi-masted fore-and-aft schooners began to show up. Many were four- or five-masted, several six-masted, and one was seven-masted. Some of them were extremely large sailing vessels that required steam winches to hoist their large gaff sails. They were at their best sailing on the wind in calm coastal waters; but they were difficult to run before the wind in hard weather. When they were used on deep-water voyages, their performance was usually much poorer than that of the square-riggers.

The gaff sail, however, soon became the most important sail for pleasure yachts. By the 17th century, the Dutch, English, and even the Swedes had gaff-rigged pleasure yachts. With the development of sport sailing and yacht clubs in the maritime nations, the gaff-rigged cutter became more and more popular, though it was sometimes surpassed in size by two- and three-masted, gaff-rigged pleasure schooners. At the beginning of the 20th century, the gaff sail was almost universally used in the yachting field.

Here, aerodynamic research performed a great service for sport sailing. As a result of new inventions, the wide gaff sail with a long boom is now almost as rare as the square sail. The only sail that has survived the extensive use of the motor yacht is the tall, narrow, gaffless boom sail, known as the Bermuda sail. Two hundred years ago, fishermen in Bermuda were using a triangular mainsail without a gaff, but with a long boom. The modern yacht uses a sail which has only the name in common with that original Bermuda sail.

SAILS IN VARIOUS SAILING VESSELS

A *Ketch*
1 Flying jib
2 Outer jib
3 Inner jib
4 Fore staysail
5 Mainsail
6 Main gaff topsail
7 Mizzen
8 Mizzen gaff topsail

B	*Four-masted barkentine*				
1	Flying jib	8	Fore lower topgallant sail	16	Mizzen
2	Outer jib	9	Fore upper topgallant sail	17	Mizzen gaff topsail
3	Inner jib	10	Main staysail	18	Jigger topmast staysail
4	Fore topmast staysail	11	Middle staysail	19	Jigger or spanker
5	Foresail	12	Main topmast staysail	20	Jigger gaff topsail
6	Fore lower topsail	13	Mainsail		
7	Fore upper topsail	14	Main gaff topsail		
		15	Mizzen topmast staysail		

C *Sloop*
1 Jib topsail
2 Jib
3 Fore staysail
4 Square foresail
5 Mainsail
6 Gaff topsail

D *Full-rigged four-masted ship*
1 Flying jib
2 Outer jib
3 Inner jib
4 Fore topmast staysail
5 Foresail
6 Fore lower topsail
7 Fore upper topsail
8 Fore topgallant sail
9 Fore royal
10 Main royal staysail
11 Main topgallant staysail
12 Main topmast staysail

13 Mainsail
14 Main lower topsail
15 Main upper topsail
16 Main topgallant sail
17 Main royal
18 Mizzen royal staysail

19 Mizzen topgallant staysail
20 Mizzen topmast staysail
21 Main spencer
22 Crossjack
23 Mizzen lower topsail
24 Mizzen upper topsail

25 Mizzen topgallant sail
26 Mizzen royal
27 Mizzen spencer
28 Jigger lower topsail
29 Jigger upper topsail
30 Jigger topgallant sail
31 Jigger royal
32 Spanker

139

THE SQUARE SAIL

A *Square-rigged mast, seen from aft*
1 Deck
2 Lower mast with top
3 Topmast with crosstrees
4 Topgallant mast
5 Royal mast
6 Pole
7 Lower yard
8 Lower topsail yard
9 Upper topsail yard
10 Topgallant yard
11 Royal yard
12 Lower sheet
13 Clewgarnet
14 Topsail clewline
15 Lower topsail buntline, shown in broken lines forward of sail
16 Topsail halliard, tie
17 Topsail halliard, spanner
18 Topsail halliard, tackle or falls
19 Upper topsail brace
20 Topsail downhaul
21 Topsail lift
22 Upper topsail yard footrope
23 Upper topsail yardarm horse
24 Topgallant sheet
25 Topgallant clewline
26 Topgallant buntline
27 Topgallant lift
28 Topgallant yard footrope
29 Royal lift
30 Royal yard footrope
31 Royal buntline

B *Plan of fife rail at mizzenmast of a big sailing ship*
1 Section of mast with spider hoop
2 Mast coat at deck
3 U-shaped fife rail with belaying pins
4 Bilge pumps on deck
5 Pump axle with flywheels
6 Detachable pump cranks stowed on fife rail
7 Chain wheel for messenger from steam winch
8 Manhole from deck to pump well
9 Fresh water pump from tanks below deck
10 Lower topsail sheet
11 Upper topsail sheet
12 Crossjack clewgarnet
13 Inner crossjack buntlines
14 Outer crossjack buntlines
15 Crossjack lift
16 Mizzen topgallant sheet
17 Main lower topgallant brace
18 Main upper topgallant brace
19 Jigger topmast staysail downhaul
20 Jigger topgallant staysail downhaul

LOWER YARD AND SAIL, WITH RUNNING GEAR, IN A BIG SQUARE-RIGGED SHIP

1 Lift by which the yard can be trimmed either way out of the horizontal. In port, this can be done independently of the yards above and to a considerable angle. At sea, when sails are set, the movement is restricted, but affects all the yards on the mast.

2 Buntline blocks under rim of top
3 Buntline blocks on yard seized to jack stay
4 Clewgarnet by which the clews of the sail are hauled up to the yardarms
5 Leech line
6 Outer buntline
7 Inner buntline
8 Middle buntline
9 Bull's eye sewn to the sail to lead the buntlines

10 Buntline hitch
11 Tacks leading forward
12 Sheets leading aft; the clews of the sail are trimmed to the wind by tacks and sheets.
When the sail is to be furled, the tacks and sheets are let go and the sail is hauled up to the yard by the clewgarnets and buntlines.

YARD WITH DETAILS

Then men go aloft, lie out on the yard, and roll up the sail tightly and secure it by tying the gaskets around yard and sail.

13 Gaskets

14 Braces leading aft, by which the yard is braced to different winds

1 Yardarm
2 Yardarm band
3 Lift shackled to yardarm band
4 Clewgarnet
5 Hauling out part of head earing
6 Round turns of head earing
7 Ring of head earing
8 Head of sail
9 Leech of sail
10 Robands, tied with a square knot
11 Jack stay

12 Clew of galvanized iron
13 Thimble for foot of sail
14 Thimble for leech
15 Shackle for sheet
16 Bull's-eye sewed into sail
17 Cringle on bolt rope with round thimble

143

RUNNING RIGGING OF THE SQUARE SAILS OF A FOUR-MASTED BARK

Braces and sheets

1 Fore brace
2 Fore lower top-
   sail brace
3 Fore upper top-
   sail brace
4 Fore lower
   topgallant brace
5 Fore upper
   topgallant brace
6 Fore royal brace
7 Main brace

8 Main lower top-
   sail brace
9 Main upper top-
   sail brace
10 Main lower
    topgallant brace
11 Main upper
    topgallant brace
12 Main royal brace
13 Crossjack brace

14 Mizzen lower
    topsail brace
15 Mizzen upper
    topsail brace
16 Mizzen lower
    topgallant brace
17 Mizzen upper
    topgallant brace
18 Mizzen royal
    brace
19 Fore sheet

20	Fore lower top-sail sheet	
21	Fore upper top-sail sheet	
22	Fore lower topgallant sheet	
23	Fore upper topgallant sheet	
24	Fore royal sheet	
25	Main sheet	
26	Main lower top-	

	sail sheet
27	Main upper top-sail sheet
28	Main lower topgallant sheet
29	Main upper topgallant sheet
30	Main royal sheet
31	Crossjack sheet
32	Mizzen lower topsail sheet

33	Mizzen upper topsail sheet
34	Mizzen lower topgallant sheet
35	Mizzen upper topgallant sheet
36	Mizzen royal sheet
37	Fore tack
38	Main tack
39	Crossjack tack

Buntlines, clewlines, and downhauls

1 Fore clewgarnet
2 Fore lower topsail clewline
3 Fore upper topsail downhaul
4 Fore lower topgallant clewline
5 Fore upper topgallant downhaul
6 Fore royal clewline
7 Main clewgarnet
8 Main lower topsail clewline
9 Main upper topsail downhaul
10 Main lower topgallant clewline
11 Main upper topgallant downhaul
12 Main royal clewline
13 Crossjack clewgarnet
14 Mizzen lower topsail clewline
15 Mizzen upper topsail downhaul
16 Mizzen lower topgallant clewline
17 Mizzen upper topgallant downhaul
18 Mizzen royal clewline
19 Fore buntlines
20 Fore lower topsail buntlines

21 Fore upper top-
    sail buntlines
22 Fore lower
    topgallant
    buntlines
23 Fore upper
    topgallant
    buntlines
24 Fore royal
    buntlines
25 Main buntlines
26 Main lower top-
    sail buntlines
27 Main upper top-
    sail buntlines

28 Main lower
    topgallant
    buntlines
29 Main upper
    topgallant
    buntlines
30 Main royal
    buntlines
31 Crossjack
    buntlines
32 Mizzen lower
    topsail buntlines
33 Mizzen upper
    topsail buntlines

34 Mizzen lower
    topgallant
    buntlines
35 Mizzen upper
    topgallant
    buntlines
36 Mizzen royal
    buntlines

EARLY METHOD OF RIGGING DOUBLE TOPSAILS, 1860

1 Lower mast, foremast	16 Topgallant sail	29 Lower topsail brace
2 Top	17 Lower studding sail	30 Lower topsail clewline
3 Cap	18 Topmast studding sail	31 Lower topsail lift
4 Topmast	19 Topgallant studding sail	32 Upper topsail sheet
5 Topmast crosstree	20 Lower rigging or shrouds	33 Upper topsail clewline
6 Lower foreyard	21 Futtock shrouds	34 Upper topsail brace
7 Lower topsail yard	22 Topmast rigging or shrouds	35 Upper topsail lift
8 Upper topsail yard	23 Lower yard footrope	36 Topgallant studding sail sheet
9 Lower studding sail yard	24 Lower topsail sheet of chain	37 Topgallant studding sail tack
10 Topmast studding sail boom	25 Inner lower studding sail halliard	38 Topmast studding sail halliard
11 Topmast studding sail yard	26 Outer lower studding sail halliard	39 Topgallant sheet
12 Topgallant studding sail boom	27 Topmast studding sail sheet	40 Topgallant clewline
13 Fore course, foresail	28 Topmast studding sail tack	
14 Lower topsail		
15 Upper topsail		

STUDDING SAILS
1 Outline sketch showing studding sails and their spars and rigging, looking aft

2 Band on the yardarm for the studding sail boom

TOPSAIL HALLIARDS AND WINCHES

A *Brace winch invented by Captain J.C. Jarvis of Tayport, Scotland. The winch controls the lower brace and the two topsail braces, one winch for each mast. The winch has three axles, each with two barrels, and is so arranged with cogwheels that when the winch is turned, braces on one side pay out as those on the other side wind on.*
1 Weather side brace paid out
2 Lee side brace hove in

B *Topsail halliard of a barkentine*
1 End of chain span across the deck
2 Mousing on hook
3 Moving block, double

4 Becket, in one with the straps
5 Fall, two-fold purchase rove to advantage
6 Pin rail
7 Belaying pin
8 Main rail

C *Topsail halliard winch*
1 Flywheel with removable handle, which was removed after the sail was hoisted so as to be out of the way
2 Worm gear
3 Grooved barrel for the halliard, tapered to increase power as the yard ascends
4 Brake

5 Wheel with threaded shaft to control the brake. When the topsail yard was lowered, the brake was eased off and the flywheel was given a start with a push. This set the barrel revolving; the downward speed was regulated by the brake.

150

151

A   *Square sail by the Rägener system*
Many inventors have tried to improve upon the traditional square rig, which evolved empirically from centuries of experience gained the hard way. None did much to improve the old sailing ship, and this system by Rägener, with trussed yards and sails running on horizontal slides and brailed in to the mast, never got beyond the drawing board.

B   *Cunningham's patent self-reefing topsail*

1   Revolving topsail yard
2   Bight of chain topsail tie
3   Topmast
4   Topsail yard parrel
5   Chafing spar to protect the sail when reefed
6   Roller lead for tie
7   Bolt for downhaul tackle
8   T-shaped bolt for the bonnet
9   Yardarm hoop within which the yard works
10   Bolt for topsail yard lifts
11   Leading block for topgallant sheet
12   Shackle to take the brace
13   Downhaul tackle
14   Twin runners of topsail halliards
15   Twin tackles of topsail halliards

153

PATENT SELF-REEFING TOPSAIL

Colling's & Pinkney's patent self-reefing topsail
1 Topsail yard
2 Parrel
3 Rolling spar
4 Iron drum end of rolling spar
5 Yardarm hoop
6 Arm carrying reefing halliard block

7 Cheek block for topgallant sheet
8 Parrel crutch with lignum vitae rollers
9 Lignum vitae rollers
10 Topsail
11 Lead block for reefing halliards
12 Topsail yardarm

DIFFERENT RIGGING OF LOWER SQUARE SAILS

A *Big square-rigged sailing ships could, sometimes, set a three-cornered mainsail or cross-jack. Such a sail could be carried in a gale long after a square sail had to be taken in, but this advantage was counteracted by* the fact that the three-cornered sail gave less spread of canvas in a moderate wind. The numbers indicate:

1 Lower yard
2 Three-cornered sail
3 Buntlines
4 Tackle sheet in front of mast

B *A four-masted bark under all sail, setting a three-cornered crossjack, while the mainsail is drawn double showing both a square sail and a three-cornered sail*

CLEWED MAINSAILS

A *A mainsail, clewed up to the yardarm, as seen from forward*
1 Lower mast
2 The top
3 Lower yard
4 Lifts
5 Lower topsail sheet, sail clewed up to the yardarm

6 The sail, say, mainsail
7 Clewgarnets
8 Buntlines
9 Leechlines
10 Tacks and sheets
11 Gaskets

B *A mainsail with the clews hauled up as seen from aft*
1 Clewgarnets
2 Buntlines
3 Leechlines
4 Sheets

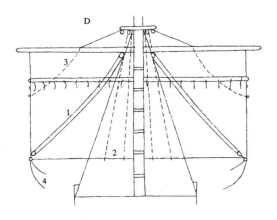

C *A mainsail
   clewed up in the
   bunt as seen from
   forward*
1 The sail
2 Reef band
3 Clewgarnets
   abaft the sail
4 Buntlines
5 Leechlines
6 Gaskets

7 Lower topsail
   sheet, sail clewed
   up in the bunt

D *A mainsail
   clewed up in the
   bunt as seen from
   aft*
1 Clewgarnets
2 Buntlines
3 Leechlines
4 Sheet

THE GAFF SAIL

1 Gaff
2 Head earing
3 Peak halliards
4 Clew shackle
5 Boom end
6 Reef cringle
7 Sheet band
8 Sheet
9 Distance line
10 Hoops
11 Bolt rope on luff of sail
12 Mast
13 Spiral lacing
14 Mainstay
15 Cap
16 Fore peak halliards
17 Peak halliard block
18 Foremast head
19 Outer jibstay
20 Outer jib halliard
21 Inner jibstay
22 Inner jib halliard
23 Forestay
24 Fore staysail halliard
25 Fore throat halliards
26 Trestletrees
27 Topmast
28 Cheeks
29 Mast battens
30 Foremast
31 Foot of sail
32 Boom
33 Seizings
34 Marline hitched lacing
35 Wire jack stay
36 Eyelet hole for lacing

THE GAFF SAIL (FROM PAASCH)

A	*Gaff sail*	8 Luff rope	15 Balance reef band
1	Throat	9 Leech	
2	Peak	10 Leech rope	16 Throat cringle
3	Tack	11 Foot	17 Peak cringle
4	Clew	12 Foot rope	18 Tack cringle
5	Head	13 First reef band	19 Clew cringle
6	Headrope	14 Second reef band	20 Reef cringles
7	Luff		21 Reef points

B *A spanker, which sets under a standing gaff and brails in to the mast (leeches and cringles made as in A)*

1 Half a cloth tabling on the luff
2 Folding on the after leech with three holes to take the brails
3 Lead of brails across the sail
4 Sheet patch
5 Tack patch
6 Peak patch
7 Detail of peak cringle

B *Another way of rigging the gaff topsail with two clewlines*

FORE-AND-AFT TOPSAILS

A	*Jib-headed gaff topsail*	5	Clewline
1	Head	6	Sheet
2	Clew	7	Throat halliard
3	Tack		of the gaff sail
4	Mast hoops	8	Peak halliard of the gaff sail

The gaff topsail is car-ried on the lee side of the peak halliard and the tack leads down to deck on the weather side of the gaff. When the ship is put about, one man has to go aloft and shift the sail over to the new lee side.

C *Different types of fore-and-aft top-sails*
1 Lateen topsail from the middle of the 16th cen-tury
2 Square gaff top-sail bent to a short yard
3 Jackyard topsail of a cutter from the 1890's

163

GAFF SAILS

GAFF SAILS

A *The peak halliards and topping lifts of the gaff sails on board a three-masted fore-and-aft schooner*

1 Fore peak halliard
2 Main peak halliard

3 Mizzen peak halliard
4 Fore topping lift
5 Main topping lift
6 Mizzen topping lift

B *The throat halliards and sheets of the gaff sails on board a three-masted fore-and-aft schooner*

1 Fore throat halliard
2 Main throat halliard

C

3 Mizzen throat
   halliard
4 Fore sheet
5 Main sheet
6 Mizzen sheet or
   spanker sheet

C *Different gaff
   sails*
1 Upper and lower
   spanker of the
   five-masted bark
   Potosi
2 Jigger of the
   four-masted bark
   Archibald Russell

3 Spanker of a big
   American fore-
   and-aft schooner.
   The vertical
   ropes (4) from
   the topping lift
   are called lazy
   jacks.

165

A

BONNETS AND REEFS

A *A merchant ship from the first half of the 17th century. Additional sails, called bonnets, are laced to the foot of her courses and lateen mizzen. Sail area can be reduced by unlacing the bonnets.*
1 Mizzen
2 Mizzen bonnet
3 Mainsail
4 Main bonnet
5 Foresail
6 Fore bonnet

B *The bonnets were laced to the sails in such a way as to make the lacing spill itself once it was started; this made quick work of shortening sail*
1 Lower sail
2 Bonnet
3 The clew of the sail seized to the earing of the bonnet
4 The leech rope of the bonnet, ending in a wall knot

and stropped to the leech of the sail
5 Lacing of head of bonnet to foot of sail is made to spill once its stop is let go

C   *Enlargement of clew of sail, showing details*

D   *Sectional view of a reefed sail*
1   Foot of sail
2   Reef band
3   Reef point
4   Reef point knotted around reef with a reef knot
5   Rolled-up canvas in reef

RUNNING GEAR OF STAYSAILS IN A FOUR-MASTED
BARK, DIFFERENT TYPES OF STAYSAILS

A *Sheets*
1 Fore royal
  staysail sheets
2 Flying jib sheets
3 Outer jib sheets
4 Inner jib sheets
5 Fore topmast
  staysail sheets
6 Main royal
  staysail sheet
7 Main topgallant
  staysail sheet
8 Main topmast
  staysail sheet
9 Mizzen royal
  staysail sheet
10 Mizzen
  topgallant
  staysail sheet
11 Mizzen topmast
  staysail sheet
12 Jigger topgallant
  staysail sheet
13 Jigger topmast
  staysail sheet
14 Jigger staysail
  sheet

B *Halliards and
  downhauls*
1 Fore royal
  staysail halliards
2 Flying jib
  halliards
3 Outer jib
  halliards
4 Inner jib
  halliards
5 Fore topmast
  staysail halliards
6 Main royal
  staysail halliards
7 Main topgallant
  staysail halliards
8 Main topmast
  staysail halliards
9 Mizzen royal
  staysail halliards
10 Mizzen
  topgallant
  staysail halliards

11 Mizzen topmast
  staysail halliards
12 Jigger topgallant
  staysail halliards
13 Jigger topmast
  staysail halliards
14 Jigger staysail
  halliards
15 Fore royal
  staysail downhaul
16 Flying jib
  downhaul
17 Outer jib
  downhaul
18 Inner jib
  downhaul
19 Fore topmast
  staysail downhaul
20 Main royal
  staysail downhaul
21 Main topgallant
  staysail downhaul
22 Main topmast
  staysail downhaul
23 Mizzen royal
  staysail downhaul
24 Mizzen
  topgallant
  staysail downhaul
25 Mizzen topmast
  staysail downhaul
26 Jigger topgallant
  staysail downhaul
27 Jigger topmast
  staysail downhaul
28 Jigger staysail
  downhaul

SAIL DETAILS

A *Norse Viking ship beating with a spar, known as a beatas, to hold the weather leech instead of a bowline; detail showing the spar's connection to sail*

B *Detail of a bowline bridle*
1 Bowline hitched to the dead block with a bowline
2 Long bridle
3 Short bridle
4 Bowline cringle in sail
5 Eyelet-holes in sail for short bridle

C *Outline drawing of an American clipper close hauled on the port tack, with her weather bowlines picked out on her courses, topsails, and topgallant sails*

D   *Section of a yard
    showing a reefed
    sail*
1   Yard
2   Jack stay
3   Stirrup
4   Sail below the
    reef
5   Reef band
6   Reefed part of
    sail

7   Reef point tied
    around yard and
    sail with a reef
    knot

E   *Bark with double
    topsails, sailing
    by the wind
    under reefed up-
    per topsails,
    lower topsails,
    and foresail*

171

BLOCKS OF DIFFERENT TYPES

1 Triple block for a hemp strop, 19th century
2 Single block, side view and front view, for a hemp strop, 18th century
3 Deadeye, 19th century
4 Clewgarnet block, side view and front view; this block has been turned on a lathe; medieval or 16th century
5 Dutch style yard-arm sheet block for topsail sheet and lower lift, front view and side view, 17th century

6 Fiddleblock, side view and front view, with two sheaves, 18th or 19th century
7 Fiddleblock, with external strap and hook, 19th century
8 Wire-stropped sheet block, with clip hooks and a cleat for the sheet, so as to make the sheet block travel on a horse, 20th century
9 Double block with a double strop and hook, for masthead pendant, 19th century

10 Triple fid-dleblock, with external strap and thimble for splicing the pendant, 19th century
11 Snatch block, with external straps and a swivel hook, 19th century

TACKLES AND BLOCKS

A   *Tackles (the number of loads indicates the increase of power for each tackle)*
1   Single whip
2   Runner
3   Gun tackle
4   Gun tackle rove to advantage
5   Luff tackle
6   Luff tackle rove to advantage
7   Double purchase

8   Double purchase rove to advantage
9   Winding tackle
10 Reversed winding tackle
11 Triple tackle
12 Reversed triple tackle
13 Four-by-three tackle
14 Three-by-four tackle
15 Four-fold tackle
16 Quadruple tackle

B   *Different blocks with internal iron straps*
1   Single block with a ring
2   Fore-and-aft jib sheet block
3   Double block with sister hooks
4   Triple block with a shackle
5   Single block with loose swivel screw eye bolt

6 Double block
   with an eye
7 Double block
   with shackle and
   becket
8 Single block with
   stiff swivel jaws
   and becket
9 Double block
   with stiff swivel
   hook and becket
10 Triple block with
   stiff fixed front
   hook and becket

11 Double block
   with eye bolt and
   nut and becket
12 Triple block with
   loose side hook
   and becket
13 Single block with
   a solid eye for
   gaff bands
14 Single block with
   stiff jaws and
   becket

15 Triple block with
   loose swivel hook
   and becket
16 Double block
   with loose swivel
   jaws with guy
   eyes
17 Double block
   with stiff swivel
   jaws with guy
   eyes and becket

SOME OLD RIGGING DETAILS

A   *Topsail, halliard,
     end of 17th cen-
     tury*
1   Tie
2   Tackle
3   Lower lift

B   *Wooden blocks without strops*
C   *Chain plate with deadeye*
D   *Block for hemp strop*
1   Shell
2   Score for the strop
3   Sheave
4   Pin

E   *Fiddleblock with one sheave smaller than the other*
F   *Deadeye, turned in a shroud*
1   Deadeye
2   Shroud
3   Throat-seizing
4   End-seizing
5   Lanyard

G   *Lower yardarm with topsail sheet block*
1   Lower yardarm
2   Topsail sheet block
3   Topsail sheet
4   Lower lift

177

TOOLS FOR SAIL-MAKING AND RIGGING WORK

1 Turning fids or heavers
2 Serving mallets
3 Big sail needle, roping needle
4 Splicing fids
5 Carved bullock's horn with tallow for holding needles
6 Prickers for small work
7 Marlinespikes for splicing wire
8 Sail-maker's palm

5

6

7

8

179

OLD TYPES OF SAILING SHIPS

 1 Egyptian sea-
    going ship, about
    1500 B.C.
 2 Roman trader,
    about A.D. 200
 3 Viking longship,
    A.D. 900
 4 Norman ship
    from the 13th
    century
 5 Hulk of the Han-
    seatic League,
    about 1470
 6 Spanish caravel,
    about 1490
 7 Spanish ship,
    nao,
    about 1490
 8 English carrack,
    about 1500
 9 North European
    boeier, 1560
10 Swedish kravel,
    galleon, 1550

OLD TYPES OF SAILING SHIPS

1 Dutch pinnace, middle of 17th century

2 Swedish packet, 1690

3 Algerian chebec, 18th century

4 Dutch flute, 1640

5 72-gun ship, 1746
6 West European
  galleon, 1590
7 Merchantman, 1770

OLD TYPES OF SAILING SHIPS

1 Swedish krayer,
   second half of
   18th century
2 Hooker, second
   half of 18th
   century
3 Swedish East
   Indiaman, 1786

4 Swedish bark, 1792
5 Swedish snow, 1783
6 Baltimore clipper, 1820

185

SOME ETHNOGRAPHICAL BOAT TYPES

1 Boat from the
  Göta River, West
  Sweden
2 Humber keel,
  Yorkshire
3 Norfolk wherry
4 Turkish caique
5 Boat from Bahia,
  Brazil

6 Sloop from
  archipelago off
  Stockholm
7 Arabian dhow
8 Fishing boat
  from the Åland
  Islands, Finland
9 Danish revenue
  cutter

10 Old barge, Lake
   of Vänern,
   Sweden

SOME ETHNOGRAPHICAL BOAT TYPES

1 Reed-boat from
  Lake Titicaca,
  South America
2 Boat from Lake
  Victoria
3 Small fishing
  boat from west
  coast of Sweden
4 Norwegian jacht
5 Boat from East
  Pakistan
6 Tartan, trading
  craft from
  western Mediter-
  ranean

7 Koster boat from
west coast of
Sweden
8 Piragua from
Tahiti

9 Portuguese
muleta
10 Boat from
Kimari, India

11 Outrigger canoe
from the South
Pacific
12 Dutch barge

SOME ETHNOGRAPHICAL BOAT TYPES

1 Dutch koff
2 Scow schooner,
   New Zealand
3 Junk, Amoy,
   South China

190

4 Paduakan, coasting craft from Celebes
5 Bovo, Sicilian coaster
6 Ketch, Åland Islands, Finland

SOME ETHNOGRAPHICAL BOAT TYPES

1 Velocera,
   Sicilian, lateen-
   rigged barkentine
2 Egyptian markab
3 Bilancella,
   Italian fishing
   craft
4 Thames barge

5 German *Heuer* boat
6 Greek fishing boat from Mykonos
7 Open Spanish fishing boat (*felucca*)
8 Small Norwegian sailing fishing boat
9 French lugger (*chasse marée*)
10 French Grand Banks schooner

DIFFERENT RIGS

1 Five-masted ship
2 Four-masted ship
3 Four-masted bark
4 Ship

5 Snow
6 Main topsail
  brigantine
7 Five-masted bark

8 Brig
9 Bark

DIFFERENT RIGS

1 Brigantine or
    hermaphrodite
    brig
2 Four-masted
    jackass bark
3 Jackass bark
4 Barkentine

5 Six-masted
    barkentine
6 Five-masted
    barkentine
7 Four-masted
    barkentine

197

DIFFERENT RIGS

1 Five-masted two-
   topsail schooner
2 Four-masted top-
   sail schooner

3 Three-masted
   topsail schooner
4 Main-topsail
   schooner or two-
   topsail schooner

5 Topsail schooner
6 Seven-masted
   fore-and-aft
   schooner

7   Four-masted fore-and-aft schooner rigged with a flying foresail

8   Three-masted fore-and-aft schooner

9   Two-masted fore-and-aft schooner

10   Three-masted staysail schooner

11   Six-masted fore-and-aft schooner

199

DIFFERENT RIGS

1 Five-masted fore-and-aft
  schooner
2 Two-masted staysail
  schooner
3 Gunter-rigged gig
4 Two-masted schooner
  with Bermuda mainsail
5 Training ship DENMARK
6 Bermuda-rigged ketch
7 Launch rigged with dip-
  ping lugsails
8 Gaff-rigged cutter
9 Baltic sloop
10 Ketch

KNOTS, WHIPPINGS, AND SPLICE

A	Overhand knot	D	Sheet bend	H	Clove hitch
B	Figure of eight knot, Flemish knot	E	Double sheet bend, variation	I	Two half-hitches
		F	Bowline	J	Fisherman's bend
C	Square knot, reef knot	G	Bowline on the bight	K	Rolling hitch
				L	Timber hitch
				M	Slippery hitch

N   *Blackwall hitch*
O   *Sheepshank*
P   *Palm and needle whipping*
Q   *Common whipping*

R   *Short splice, ropes put together before beginning to splice*

SWEDISH FLAGS

1 In the second
half of the 16th
century the pres-
ent Swedish flag
was not yet in
use. Instead
Swedish men-of-
war flew a blue-
and-white striped
flag.
The pennant at
the masthead,
however, carried
the three Swedish
crowns.
2 The three-
tongued blue flag
of the fleet of the
army, 1761–1813
3 The ensign of
1658, from the
oldest preserved
Swedish flag,
now in the
Rijksmuseum,
Amsterdam
4 Merchant flag,
1815–1844, with
the canton of the
Swedish-Nor-
wegian Union
5 The ensign with
the canton of the
Union, 1844–
1905
6 Merchant flag,
after 1905

3

4

5

6

SIGNAL FLAGS

*Earlier signal systems
During a few decades
in the middle of the
19th century, Maryat's
code was in use before
the Commercial Code
became universal.
The number in Mar-
ryat's code of the
Swedish three-masted
ship* Indiaman *of Gä-
vle, 1856, is shown
above the ship.*

SPLICES

When splicing cordage the strands are tucked against the lay. Each strand is taken over the strand on its left and then under the next one.

A *Long splice*
1 The ropes laid up before beginning to splice
2 Way of knotting the strands
3 Way of tucking the strands

B *Eye splice*
1 Way of placing the strand before commencing the splice
2 Way of tucking the two first strands

C *Eye splice on a wire rope, one tuck made on each strand.*

When splicing wire rope each strand is generally tucked around the same strand all the time, in the same direction, as the single wires are laid.

A1

A2

A5

A3

A4

B

A   *Great Britain*
1   Union flag
2   Cross of St. George
3   Cross of St. Andrew
4   Cross of St. Patrick

5   Merchant flag (red ensign)
B   According to a legend, the Danish flag fell from the sky in front of the army in 1219 and led

the army to victory. It is probably the oldest flag in the world, and has been Denmark's colors since the 14th century.

208

C1

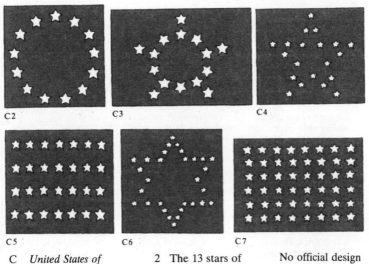

C2   C3   C4

C5   C6   C7

C *United States of America*
1 The U.S. flag of today. The stars represent the 50 states and the stripes the original 13 states

2 The 13 stars of 1777
3 1795
4 1818
5 1846
6 1848
7 1912

No official design for placement of the stars existed before 1912

FLAGS

House flags from sailing ship days

1 The Hanseatic League, Lübeck (the Middle Ages)
2 The East India Company, London
3 Black Ball Line, New York (1816)
4 Enoch Train White Diamond Line, Boston (1820's)
5 Grinnell, Minturn & Co., New York, Swallow Tail Line for Liverpool
6 Grinnell, Minturn & Co., New York, Swallow Tail Line for London
7 Arthur Sewall, Bath, Me.
8 Alaska Packers Association, San Francisco
9 Money Wigram & Sons, London
10 George Thompson & Co., Aberdeen White Star Line, Aberdeen
11 John Willis & Son, London
12 Devitt & Moore, London
13 John Hardie & Co., Glasgow
14 Thomas Law & Co., Shire Line, Glasgow
15 John Stewart & Co., London
16 Andrew Weir & Co., Bank Line, Glasgow
17 Soc. Anon. Des Voiliers Nantais, Nantes
18 Ferdinand Laeisz, Hamburg
19 S.O. Stray & Co., Kristiansand
20 Gustaf Erikson, Mariehamn

An old engraving shows Magellan during his trip around the world, 1519–1522. Magellan was never able to complete this first circumnavigation of the globe himself, and of the original five vessels, with 265 men in the crew, only one ship, the VIC-TORIA, and eighteen men returned. The engraving introduces the chapter on navigation and ship-handling.

NAVIGATION AND SHIP-HANDLING
by Rolf Scheen

T he art of determining the position and course of a ship and thus guiding it from port to port is known as navigation, from the Latin *navis,* a ship, and *agere,* to drive. In order to navigate successfully, the sailor must be able to determine three things: *(1)* the actual position of the ports of departure and destination; *(2)* the course the ship must take in order to reach its port of destination safely; *(3)* how far the ship has sailed since leaving port.

The first act of navigation took place some time in the dawn of history and probably then did not involve the primitive craft leaving one place bound for a specific destination. The object of the voyage was, almost certainly, to cross a body of water, such as a river, a lake, or a bay. When the urge to explore came, or when the need to find food, game, or living space arose, the land on the other side of the water was one of the places first considered. Once it had been established that it was indeed possible to cross over the water in the primitive craft available, the problem of finding the way home arose. And if the newly explored land was considered to be worth returning to, the sailor would want to be able to find it again. Just as migratory birds have developed the ability to find their way south in winter and north in summer, always to the same places, year after year, so did early man develop his sense of direction and perception, so that he could find his way without any mechanical aids. This ability is noticeable even today in older fishermen who seem to have developed the ability to "smell" their way round their home waters. But it is among the primitive peoples of the world that this ability is best seen today. The Eskimo, for instance, can find his way home in his kayak through darkness and storms, guided only by his instinct. Early sailors, who had no mechanical aids to guide them, developed this instinctual sense of position, assisted by a keen perception that noted the relevance of current flow, flotsam from land, and the flight of seabirds.

However, even if we consider the sailors of the Stone and Bronze Ages to have been excellent practitioners of primitive navigation, no real step forward in the art could be achieved until the science of mathematics had advanced considerably. And although astronomy was considered a science in Babylon in the third millennium before our era, and Chinese scholars could compute the occurrence of solar eclipses, this knowledge was not applied to navigation. One reason for this could be that at that time there was no pressing need for such development, as most shipping that took place then consisted of river traffic. It was first the Phoenicians and then the Greeks who began sailing out of sight of land and therefore needed to develop navigation as a science.

For a long time, however, coastal navigation remained the dominant form of shipping in the Mediterranean basin. By coastal navigation is meant that the ship, if at all possible, never went out of sight of land, the sailor's most important navigational instrument being, therefore, the eyes.

The first navigational aid to be developed was the lead and line, and this is recorded in ancient Egypt, where shipping on the Nile represented a vital means of transport. The Nile waters can be so turbid that it is impossible to see the bottom, and annual flooding alters the river's course so that banks and shoals change place regularly. Therefore, the Nile rivermen had to be able to sound the river. Some ancient depictions of Egyptian boats show a man in the prow using a long pole to measure the depth of the water. On larger boats, the hull's height above the water made poles impractical, and the lead and line came into use. In the year 62 A.D., the ship that foundered when taking the apostle Paul as prisoner to Rome is recorded as having a lead. By that time, the lead was so developed that the line was marked in fathoms.

The main object of the lead was to save the ship from going aground. Once the position of a shoal or bank was known, it could be avoided. Landmarks, or transit marks, were noted, so that transit lines could be followed, thus keeping the ship clear of danger. Transit lines are used today still in coastal navigation.

Once the art of writing became widespread, information about navigational dangers was gathered and noted down for use by mariners. Greek and Phoenician scholars were especially proficient at this, writing down sailing directions and navigational information on what were called *peripli*. Herodotus (*c.* 450 B.C.) tells us that King Darius I of Persia hired Phoenician ships to spy on the Greek coast and to make up a set of sailing

THE OLD LOG WITH A LINE AND GLASS

The chip log is an old instrument for measuring the speed of a ship. It consists of a flat piece of wood formed as a sector of a circle and weighted to enable it to float upright, secured to a line so as to make it float square. When thrown overboard it will remain stationary in the water and, as the ship sails away, the measured line will reel off at a corresponding rate. An hourglass determines the fixed interval of time, and the length of line run out will measure the speed of the ship. A quick pull on the line will detach the peg in the log chip, making it float flat so it can be hauled in.

1 The log, known as the wood float or chip
2 Lead pellets holding the chip vertically in the water
3 Wooden peg, which allows the chip to float flat when it is pulled out
4 Log-line measured off in "knots," having a similar relation to a nautical mile as the trickle of sand in the hourglass has to one hour
5 Log reel
6 Mark for two knots and a plain mark for half a knot
7 Hourglass, log glass, running for 28 seconds. A 14-second glass is used for speeds over 8 knots

directions for his navy, for use when it would be navigating Greek waters.

Later on, sea charts became more important than sailing directions, but they could not become truly useful until the invention and widespread acceptance of the compass. The first known map of the world to have a grid of lengthwise and crosswise lines was that drawn by Eratosthenes, who was head of the famous Library at Alexandria in the second century B.C. Map-making developed through the centuries, and in 1569, Gerard Mercator, a Flemish cartographer, invented a special grid called the Mercator projection, which he used when drawing maps. On the Mercator projection, the globe is represented as a cylinder with the lines of longitude parallel to each other. As a result, it was possible to draw a correct course line between two points on the map. The scale of the map varied from the Equator to the poles, so that at 60 degrees North or South, for instance, one nautical mile on the chart had twice the length of the nautical mile at the Equator. In the neighborhood of the poles, the Mercator projection cannot be used at all.

On a map, the distance from the Equator to the poles is divided into 90 degrees of latitude (North or South). The Equator itself is divided into 360 degrees of longitude, with a vertical (a meridian, or a line of longitude) stretching from each degree to the poles. In the beginning, no 0-meridian was considered standard, and each country placed it where they thought fit, often picking their own capital city as the point through which the 0-meridian passed. In 1634, King Louis XIII of France decreed that the 0-meridian was to be considered as passing through the island of Ferro, the most westerly of the Canary Islands, then regarded as the Old World's most westerly point. This was used internationally until 1884, when it was agreed that the 0-meridian was to be considered as passing through the Greenwich Observatory (founded in 1675), which is situated in the outskirts of London.

In ancient times, a great deal of courage was required of mariners who ventured so far out to sea that the land "fell away" from view. No reliable charts existed then; nor did the compass. Perhaps it was a combination of good weather, the spirit of adventure, curiosity, and the improving seaworthiness

THE LEAD

A *Egyptian boat model with oarsmen, helmsman, and leadsman (from a grave sediment, 2060-1730 B.C.)*

B,C *Deep-sea lead 16 to 20 lbs. The lower end of the lead, C2, is hollowed out, 3, to receive an arming of tallow on which samples of the sea bed are brought up for examination.*

D *Deep-sea lead of cast iron*

HAND LEAD AND LINE

The lead is the sailor's oldest navigational instrument, known even in ancient Egypt. It consists of a lead weight and a measured line, which is used to determine the depth of water. For different depths, leads of different weights were used, but today the deep-sea lead is replaced by sounding machines or echo sounders. The hand lead is still used occasionally in shallow water. The line used to be 20 fathoms long, and in the Royal British Navy it is marked in the following way:

2 fathoms: two strips of leather

3 fathoms: three strips of leather

5 fathoms: a piece of white duck

7 fathoms: a piece of red bunting

10 fathoms: a piece of leather with a hole in it

13 fathoms: a piece of blue serge

15 fathoms: a piece of white duck

17 fathoms: a piece of red bunting

20 fathoms: a piece of house line with two knots

219

OLD NAVIGATIONAL INSTRUMENTS

A Astrolabe, constructed by the Arabs in the 10th century, and used, mostly by the Spaniards and Portuguese, up to the 17th century. It consists of a freely suspended graduated ring with a diametrical ruler holding two sight vanes through which the sun or a star may be observed, the altitude being read off on the circle.

B The fore staff is composed of a square staff and three vanes of different lengths. The sides of the staff have different scales, each corresponding to one of the vanes. When observing the altitude of the sun (star) only one vane is used. Holding one end of the staff to his eye, the observer moves the vane until he sees its lower end level with the horizon and the upper end in one with the sun. The altitude is read off where the vane cuts the staff.

C   Davis' quadrant is composed of two arcs of a circle having the same center and three vanes: the horizon vane (1) with a slot, the shade vane (2), and the sight vane (3) with a sight hole. The horizon vane is fixed at the cen- ter, the other two vanes run upon the arcs. The quadrant is used with the obser- ver's back to the sun. The shade vane is set at a suitable number of degrees, and the observer moves the sight vane until he ob- serves the sun's shadow in one with the horizon, as seen through the slot in the horizon vane.

D   Gunter's quadrant is made on the same prin- ciples as the Davis' quadrant, and it is used with the obser- ver's back to the sun.

221

of their ships that persuaded them to sail onward, even though land had long since vanished from view. The regularity of the prevailing winds in the Indian Ocean, where the summer monsoon winds blow south-west and the winter monsoon winds blow north-east, made it a favourable ocean for voyages without instruments. The first European to use these winds is believed to have been Hippalos, a Greek mariner, although the Arabs and Indians had used them for centuries before that.

As daring sea expeditions, however, the great voyages of the Vikings through the mists and storms of the North Atlantic to Iceland, Greenland, and North America must be said to rank high. Admittedly, the Vikings had quite a good knowledge of the movements of the celestial bodies and could use this knowledge in navigating their way to distant places and back. The apparent movements of the sun across the sky, and of the Little Dipper and the North Star by night were important aids in helping them navigate. The bright summer nights and the Midnight Sun also played a part in Viking seamanship. Many astronomical terms from Viking times have survived, but their meaning is lost in the mists of time.

It has long been possible to determine latitude with a fair amount of certainty, but finding longitude at sea was an almost insoluble problem due to the lack of an instrument to measure time accurately. On land, it was possible to work out longitude by a very complicated and time-consuming system that was too difficult to use on board ship. A chronometer that would keep exact time throughout a long ocean voyage was needed. In 1714, the British government offered a reward of 20,000 pounds, an enormous sum in those days, to anyone who perfected such a chronometer. In 1759, John Harrison, a Yorkshire clockmaker, perfected a marine chronometer that was tested on two voyages to Jamaica. After six weeks at sea, the clock erred by only five seconds. With Harrison's chronometer, a revolution in navigation took place; from then on, it was possible to determine the longitude of a ship's position at sea. In 1774, Harrison received the prize for his great contribution to navigation.

The most important innovation in the history of navigation is much older, however, and this is the invention of the compass. The first use of the magnetic compass has been attributed to the ancient Chinese of the Hsia Dynasty (*c.* 2600 B.C.), although this now seems unlikely. The earliest Chinese reference to the use of a compass on board a ship seems to be in a document from 1111 A.D., and it is possible that the Chinese had their first contact with the compass from Indian seamen. According to Are Frode, the Vikings used a *leiderstein* (lodestone) as a primitive compass during a voyage from Norway to Iceland in 868 A.D. Considering the huge quantities of magnetite to be found in Norway, it is not unreasonable to suppose that the Norwegians discovered its properties at an early stage and had conceived the idea of using magnetite aboard ship to help them to establish the position of North.

Celestial navigation is based upon the measurement of the altitude of celestial bodies and the determination of their position. All ships measuring the height of the same celestial body at the same time and finding the same height are placed on the same astronomical position line. This fact can be used to establish position according to principles first laid down in 1837 by the American naval officer, Thomas H. Sumner, and further amplified by Marc St. Hilaire around 1875. Many different instruments have, in the course of time, been invented to measure the altitude of celestial bodies: the quadrant is said to have been invented by the Greek astronomer Hipparchos as early as the year 150 B.C. The Jacob's staff, or the cross-staff, was invented by Levi Ben Gerson from Catalonia in 1342. John Hadley constructed the Hadley quadrant in 1731, and this was soon developed into the sextant by the British naval officer Campbell in 1757.

A number of computed tables is necessary in order to establish position through celestial navigation. Such tables were first published in 1475 under the title *Ephemerides Astronomicae* by Regiomontanus. In 1755, Tobias Mayer, a German scientist living in Göttingen, edited tables necessary for establishing Greenwich Mean Time. Then, in 1767, the *British Nautical Almanac* was compiled by Nevil Maskelyne, the Astronomer Royal, and it has been published regularly since then.

When laying a course, the navigator must draw a line from the position of the port of departure to that of the port of destination. The course can then be read by placing a compass along

OCTANT AND SEXTANT

Hadley's octant, invented in 1731, and a forerunner of the sextant. The octant brought the art of measuring altitudes at sea to theoretical perfection, and later improvements are due to better methods of manufacturing only.

The sextant (opposite) is an improvement on Hadley's octant, which is said to have been invented in 1731. The sextant is a portable, reflecting astronomical instrument for measuring angles. When used, it can be held in the hand without a stand, which is essential on board ships at sea. The instrument consists of a sector-shaped frame with a graduated arc of a circle. Pivoted at the center of the arc is a radius bar, which swings across the surface of the graduated arc. The principal parts of a sextant are:

1 The frame
2 The arc, known as the limb
3 The index bar
4 Clamping mechanism
5 Micrometer screw
6 Index mirror
7 Horizon glass
8 Telescope
9 Index shades
10 Horizon shades
11 Measured angle
12 Reading of measured angle, here 45° O'

the line, taking into account the variation caused by the fact that the geographic North Pole and the magnetic North Pole have different positions. Consideration must also be taken of the built-in magnetism of the ship, which depends on the amount of iron in the ship, her machinery, and the cargo, as this causes a deviation on the compass.

Before the advent of charts which gave exact distances, it was very difficult to determine accurately how far a ship had sailed during a certain span of time. In ancient times, when ships were propelled by oars, distance was measured roughly by keeping count of the amount of time the rowers were active. On board sailing-ships, the hand log and hourglass were used, but this only gave the speed at the time of logging, so that distances sailed over longer periods of time could not be measured accurately.

A traverse board was used to record the direction and approximate distance sailed on different tacks. When the log book came into use, this information was entered in it, and account was taken of such factors as drift due to currents, etc.

The thousands upon thousands of shipwrecks lying on the sea bed all over the world bear silent witness to the dangers that have plagued mariners since earliest times. During its long history, before it was phased out of the world's shipping lanes by the engine-powered vessel, the sailing-ship went through a long period of development. In that time, the ship became bigger, more seaworthy, and could sail farther, necessitating the development of the art of navigation from the simple forms it had in the Middle East to the advanced forms it took at the end of the era. Today, the sailing-ship is no more, but the art of navigation has progressed beyond the wildest dreams of the early mariners, with the use of electronics and satellites, while the word "navigation" now means the science of determining position and course on land, on water, in the air, and in space.

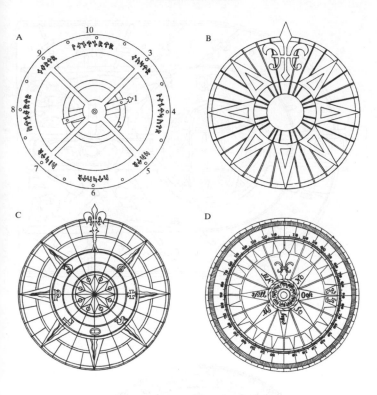

OLD COMPASS CARDS

A *Compass, 13th century*
Reconstruction of a Scandinavian compass (leidarstein) with a bronze bowl and a wooden float, with a lodestone to point the compass

1 Lid forming a cross with a center hole controlling the float

2 Float with lodestone

3 AUSTR, east

4 LANDSUDR, southeast

5 SUDR, south

6 UTSUDR, southwest

7 VESTR, west

8 UTNORDR, northwest

9 NORDR, north

10 LANDNORDR, northeast

B *Compass card, 1345*

C *Compass card, 1545*

D *Compass card, end of the 18th century*

227

A

B

C

EARLY NAVIGATIONAL INSTRUMENTS

A *Pocket sun-dial, 1453. The indicator, which cast the sun's shadow on the figures, is under the lid in the middle.*

B *Nocturne, 1580, to tell the time from the stars.*

C *Traverse board, to record the direction and distance made on tacks during a watch.*

BEARINGS

A *Reconstruction of a compass card from the Viking Age*
B *Pelorus*
1, 2   Sight vanes
3   Position line
4   Object
5   Fore-and-aft mark to which the ship's course on the pelorus is clamped
6   Compass bearing
C *Cross bearing*
  The exact position of the ship (1) will be known if bearings of two objects (2 and 3) are taken at the same time

D *Distance by four-point bearing*
  When a fixed object (2) is bearing 45 degrees on the bow (3) note the time or log. Then the same course is steered until the object bears on the beam, or 90 degrees from the course (4). The distance (6) run by the ship (1) in the interval is the distance (7) of the object when abeam. This is clear from the fact that the ship's course and the two bearings form an isosceles triangle (3, 4, 5), where the two sides (6, 7) are equal.

231

LIGHTHOUSES

A   *Open coal fire at Djursten, Sweden, 1765*

B   *Fire on tilting spar, 1635*

C   *Modern caisson lighthouse, built of concrete on shore, launched, and towed to its station and there sunk*

D   *Pharos at Alexandria, 300 B.C.*

E   *Torre de Herculum at Coruna, at the time of Christ*

F   *Tour d'Ordre at Boulogne, A.D. 40*

233

A   *Cordouan at the mouth of Girande estuary in France, 1610*
B   *Eddystone light in the Channel*
1   *1698 (at low water)*
2   *1759 (at low water)*
3   *1882 (at high water)*

C *Lighthouse lamp
for paraffin oil
with 4 wicks,
1880's*

A

Its die Caer
te vander See om oost eñ
west te seplen/eñ is vandie beste Piloots/
eñ is wt die aldervetste Caerten gecorrigeert
diemen weet te vinden/eñ elcke cust opzün ge
stelt/verbetert eñ vermeerdert met veel scho
ne figueren daer up gemaect. Eñ ooc sal men
hier in vinde wat een man van node is omme
Stuermanschap te leren. Anno.1561.

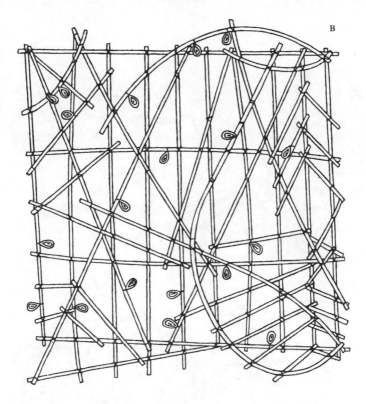

B

CHARTS

Verbal descriptions have probably existed as long as man has sailed. The oldest written "pilots" are the Greek Periples which gave distances and courses (about 300 B.C.). These were the origins of the Roman Portulanes. In the 15th and 16th centuries, "pilots" were published in most West European countries.

A The title page of the Dutch "Het Leeskaartboek van Wisboy" (the "Chart book" from Visby), first published in 1551. Several editions followed in Dutch as well as in German. The book also contained woodcut shore views. This figure is from the edition of 1561.

B Native chart of the Marshall Islands consisting of a framework of palmleaf veins with shells or coral pieces indicating the different islands and their relative positions. The distances between the islands were not always known, but most important were the directions.

A

CHARTS AND SURVEYING

A *Detail from a*   B *A Swedish chart*
Swedish chart of   *of the Sound,*
the Baltic, 1645   *1819; the same*
                       region is shown
                       in the upper part
                       of A

B

THEORY OF SAILING

A   *A boat beating to windward*
1   Sail
2   The force and direction of the wind, which can be resolved into the two components, 3 and 4
3   This force blowing parallel to the sail may be disregarded
4   This force can be resolved into two components, 5 and 6
5   This force works abeam and tends to heel the boat and to drive it to leeward. This tendency, however, is largely overcome by the lateral resistance of the water on the boat's hull and keel.
6   Of the original wind force, it is this component only that carries the boat ahead.

B   *Reaching; the wind abeam*
When the wind is abeam the lateral component (1) is reduced and the fore-and-aft component (2) is increased. The boat moves faster than when beating to windward (A).

C   *Running*
When running, the sails must not be at right angles to the direction of the wind
1   Mainsail
2   Spinnaker

D *Center of effort*
Every sail has a center of effort (1). The center of effort of the total sail area (2) is obtained by combining the centers of each sail. Theoretically, if the center of effort is ahead of the center of lateral resistance (3), the boat will tend to pay off from the wind. If 2 is abaft 3, the boat will tend to come up into the wind. In reality, the boat, when sailing, is heeling to leeward and the force of the wind will be applied at the center of effort on the lee side of the boat and cause her to luff. To counteract this, the center of effort of the sails is always placed forward of the center of lateral resistance, as shown above.

THE SET OF SAILS

A *A square-rigged vessel beating to windward*
In a square-rigger sailing on the wind the lower yards are always braced up more than the upper yards. The reason for this is that the lower sails cannot be set as flat as the upper sails, and thus require a broader wind to fill them than the small sails. Again, should the wind shift and the ship be caught aback, the upper sails will back first and warn the ship in time so that she can be paid off.

242

C

B   *The lead of the*
    fore staysail sheet
1   There must be
    sufficient gap
    between the fore
    staysail and the
    mainsail, other-
    wise (as in the
    figure) the driv-
    ing force of the
    mainsail will be
    reduced

2   A fore staysail
    which is correctly
    sheeted increases
    the suction on
    the lee side of
    the mainsail and
    thus increases its
    power

C   *Unsteady wind*
    A squall
    generally blows
    in a fan-shaped
    pattern. In spite
    of paying-off at
    the beginning
    and then luffing,
    the squall may be
    used to bring the
    boat to windward
    of her first track.

A BARK SAILING ON DIFFERENT COURSES

1 Bark sailing on the wind on the starboard tack
2 Sailing, reaching with wind abeam on the starboard side
3 Going large with the wind abaft the beam on the starboard side
4 Running free with the wind on the starboard quarter
5 Running before the wind; the wind is on the starboard side; headsails are partly blanketed, some staysails are furled
6 Running dead before the wind, scudding in a gale; spanker is furled, staysails not drawing, the headsails are blanketed
7 Running before the wind; wind is on the port side. Headsails are partly blanketed, some staysails are furled
8 Running free with the wind on the port quarter
9 Going large, sailing with a fair wind, with the wind abaft the beam on the port side
10 Sailing, reaching with the wind abeam on the port side
11 Sailing on the wind on the port tack

SMALL-BOAT HANDLING

To fetch a buoy
1 Sails set to the wind
2 Luff and trim sails to the wind
3 Luff and flatten in the sails

4 Luff as much as possible and spill the wind from the foresail and mainsail

5 Steer close to windward of the buoy and carefully judge the speed of approach

SMALL-BOAT HANDLING

A   *Going about*
1   Keep her full and by
2   "Helm's alee"
3   Flatten the foresail (applicable to dull-turning boats only)
4   Haul the foresail over and trim sheets by the wind on the new tack

B   *Jibing*
1   Boat steering before the wind; you want to take the wind on the port quarter
2   Luff a little and shorten your sheets
3   By ready to jibe
4   Up helm; jibe easily and let the sheets run
5   Meet her and trim yaw sails

A SQUARE-RIGGED VESSEL, A THREE-MASTED BARK, WEARING

1 The bark is sailing on the wind on the starboard tack.

2 "Ready to wear ship!" The mainsail is clewed up and the braces are coiled down for running.

3 The spanker is furled. "Up helm!" "Square in the mainyard!" The wheel is put to port and the mainyard is squared.

4 Without sail aft the vessel is paying off.

5 The bark is before the wind. "Round forward!" The headsails are braced around and the jibs sheeted over to starboard.

6 When she is coming up on the new tack the headsails will meet her. The after yards are braced up.

7 The spanker is set and all sails are trimmed by the wind.

8 The bark is kept on the wind on the port tack. The main sail is set and the deck cleared up.

A SQUARE-RIGGED VESSEL, A THREE-MASTED BARK, TACKING

1 The bark is sailing on the wind on the port tack. "Ready about!"

2 She is kept off a little to make all sails draw better to increase the speed.

3 "Helm's alee!" The wheel is put down, the headsheets are let go to make the jibs spill the wind; the spanker is hauled aweather to assist the luffing.

4 The bark is nearly into the wind. Now "Mainsail haul!" The mainyards are braced around, the jibs are hauled over and sheeted home, while the vessel is head in the wind.

5 The movement ahead is decreasing. With the headsails aback the bark is forced over to port.

6 When the sails of the mainmast begin to fill, the order is, "Let go and haul!" and the headsails are hauled around.

7 The vessel is paying off until the sails are filling. All sails are trimmed by the wind.

8 The bark is going ahead, the wake is becoming normal.

9 She is kept on the wind on the starboard tack; the running gear is coiled down.

A SAILING VESSEL, A BRIG, BACKING AND FILLING DOWN A RIVER WITH THE EBB TIDE, AGAINST A HEADWIND. SHE HAS ONLY THE TOPSAILS SET.

1 The brig is filling both topsails to make her move ahead to keep her in the fairway.

2 Backing the mainyard stops her progress and makes her drift broadside downriver.

3 Backing all makes her take a stern board.

4 By pointing the yards into the wind she is made to stand still and drift with the ebb tide.

5 Filling the fore topsail makes her draw ahead.

6 Filling all makes her go ahead more.

7 She is kept off a little to increase her movement through the water.

8 She is making sail, and trims them by the wind.

9 She is clear of the river and stands to sea under all sail on the starboard tack.

10 Wind direction

11 The ebb tide

TO HEAVE TO AND TO GOOSE-WING A SAIL

When a sailing ship was in a contrary gale of wind the order to heave to meant that most of sails were taken in and the helm was put down. This kept the ship's head to the wind, and, with the sea on the bow, she would ride well enough as long as some sail could be carried. This full-rigged ship has the fore topmast staysail and the goose-winged main lower topsail set. To furl the weather half of a lower topsail

was the last resource to shorten sail without having to furl all and drift under bare poles. The large scale drawing shows a part of the main mast with the goose-winged lower topsail. The numbers indicate:

1 Main mast
2 Heel of topmast
3 Mainyard with mainsail furled
4 Upper topsail yard with topsail furled
5 Lower topsail yard
6 Goose-winged lower topsail
7 Heavy lashing on sail, parceled to protect sail from chafe
8 Size of lower topsail when set
9 Lower topsail buntlines
10 Lower topsail clewlines

MOORING AND BELAYING

A   *Bitts*
B   *Knightheads*
C   *Bitts on the forecastle head*
D   *Knighthead*
    A-D are from a book on ship building by Å.C. Rålamb (1691)
E   *Belaying to a single bollard*
F   *Belaying to twin bollards*
1   Racked turns
G   *Stoppering a rope*
    Stoppers are used when hawsers are to be moved from the winch to the bollards, chain stoppers are used on wires
H   *Two berthing hawsers on the same bollard on shore*
1   Wrong way, the second hawser will block the first one
2   Right way, either of the hawsers can be removed from the bollard independently of the other

I   *Berthing hawsers*
1   Stern rope
2   After breast rope
3   After back spring
4   Fore back spring
5   Fore breast rope
6   Head rope

This picture of a rope-yard is taken from the classic nautical volume Allgemeines Wörterbuch der Marine by J.H. Röding, published in 1798.

Index

INDEX

accommodations for crew 22
   23 66 67
anchors *52–55* 58
astrolabe *220*

bell *60 63*
block and tackle *172–175*
bonnets *166*
bowsprit 76 77 *100–101*
   114–117 133

capstan *57*
carpenter's tools 10 *37–39*
charts 217 *236–239*
chronometer 222
compass *222–223* 226 *227*
   cards *227 230*
composite ship *27* 29
cross-staff *220* 223

decoration of ships 28
   46–51
deck 21 26 27 *31*
donkey boiler 59

emergency tiller *45*
engines 10 29 85 226
ethnographical boat types
   186–193

flags 11 12 *204–206 208–*
   211
forecastle 20 22 24

galleys *64–65*

halliard-and-brace 59
horn and whistle *62*
hourglass *61 216* 226
house flags *210–211*
hulls 16 17 20 21 *22* 24 25
   28 29 32

joints 24 *30*

keel 17 *18–19* 24 25 *26–*
   27 29 30 *33 34 35 36*
knots *202–203*

lanterns *70–71*
lanyard 76 84
lead and line 215 *218–219*
lifeboats *68–69*
light houses *232–235*
lines of a sailing ship *22–23*
log *216* 226
log book 226

masts 76 77 82 83 *85–101*
   136
   foremast 19 *34* 78 82 83
      86 87 88 89
   mainmast 19 *78* 82 83 85
      86 87 88 89 125
   mizzenmast 19 *33* 35 78 8
      82 83 85 86 87 88 89 14
midship sections *26 27*

navigation 13 214 215 217 22
   223 226 231

octant 13 *224*

parrels *106*
pumps *72–73*

quadrant *221*

reefing *152–153 154*
rigging 10–11 76 77 81 84
   102–121 176–177
rudders 20 *33* 35 *40–43*
   44 45

running gear *142 144–147 169*

sailing, theory of *240–246*
  backing and filling 13 *249*
  heaving to *250*
  mooring *251*
  tacking *248*
  wearing *247*
sailmaking tools *178–179*
sails 124–176
  Bermuda sail 137
  double topsails 84 *148 171*
  flying jib 81
  fore-and-aft sails 124 128 129 132 136
  fore staysail 129
  fore topmast staysail 132
  gaff sails 136 137 *158–165*
  jib sails 132
  lateen 20 21 125 127 128 192
  lower yard *142 143*
  lug sails 129 132
  main *131 134 135 138 139 156 157*
  main staysail 132
  main topmast sail 132
  mizzen staysail 132
  self-reefing topsail *153 154*
  spritsails 126 129 136
  staysails 80 81 82 *168–169*
  studding sails 133
  topgallant sail 80 82 132 133 136
  topsail 11 77 80 84 125
  Viking sails 125
shipbuilding
  carvel 8 9
  clinker 8 9 17 24
  iron 10 29

shell 16 17
skeleton 16 17
ships, types of
  ancient and medieval 16–17 20–21 24 40 43 180–181
  Baltimore clipper 25 27 28 *82 185*
  barge, Dutch *189*
  barge, Thames *192*
  barge, Vänern (Sweden) *187*
  bark *11 35* 66 *78–79 83 87 94 95 96 102–103 130–131 144–145 155* 165 *168 171 185 195 196 244 247*
  barkentine 46 66 *88 90* 137 *138 150 192 196–197*
  bilancella, Italian fishing boat *192*
  boeier, N. Europe *181*
  boat
    Bahia (Brazil) *186*
    East Pakistan *188*
    Kimari (India) *189*
  bovo (Sicilian coaster) *191*
  brig *88 134 195 196 249*
  brigantine 51 *88 195 196*
  caique (Turkish) *186*
  caravel 24
    Spanish *181*
  carrack 24
    English *181*
  Chasse Marée 129 *193*
  chebec (Algerian) *182*
  clipper 28 *83 96* 133 *170*
  cog 24
  cutter 137 163 *201*
  dhow (Arabian) 128 *187*
  East Indiaman

(Swedish) *184*
Egyptian 16 17 *180 218*
felucca (Spanish) *193*
fishing boats
  Mykonos (Greece) *193*
  Norwegian *193*
  Swedish *188*
  Åland (Finland) *187*
fleut (Dutch) *43 182*
frigate *33 34* 80 *111*
galiot 24
galleas 24
galleon 24 *181 183*
gig *138 200*
Göta River boat (Swedish)
  186
Grand Banks schooner 193
Heuer (German) *193*
hooker *184*
hulk *180*
Humber keel (English)*187*
jacht (Norwegian) *188*
junk (Chinese) *50 190*
ketch *90 138 191 201*
koff (Dutch) *190*
Koster boat (Swedish) *189*
kravel (Swedish) *181*
krayer (Swedish) *184*
Lake Victoria boat (Africa)
  188
lugger (French) *193*
man-of-war 81
markab (Egyptian) *192*
merchantman 81 *166 183*
muleta (Portuguese) *189*
nao (Spanish) *123 181*
Norfolk wherry (English)
  186
Norman boat *180*
outrigger canoe (South
  Pacific) *189*
paduakan (Celebes

coaster) *191*
  piragua (Tahitian) *189*
  pinnace (Dutch) 46 *50 18*
  reed boat, Lake Titicaca
    188
  Roman ships
    17 20 *40 180*
  scow schooner (New
    Zealand) *190*
  schooner 46 73 82 *85 88*
    89 90 92–93 120 *134*
    135 137 164 165 *193*
    198–200
  72-gun ship *183*
  ship of the line 80 *119*
  sloop 80 *90 139 186 200*
  snow *94 118 183*
  steamers *10* 28 29 *120 121*
  tartan (Mediterranean) *1*
  velocera (Sicilian) *192*
  Viking ship 17 25 *26* 28
    40 55 180
  wood-and-iron 9 10 27 *29*
  yawl 90
spars *76–99*
stays and shrouds *104–105*
splices *203 207*
sun-dial *228*

tops *100 101 107*

whistles *62*
winch 58 59 84 137 150
  151
windlass *56 58*

yachts 10 29 137